What Are We Doi

What
Are We Doing
When We Pray?

A Philosophical Inquiry

Vincent Brümmer

SCM PRESS LTD

Brümmer, Vincent
 What are we doing when we pray?
 1. Prayer
 I. Title
 291.4'3   BV210.2

ISBN 0-334-02421-8

334 02421 8

First published 1984
by SCM Press Ltd
26–30 Tottenham Road, London N1

Typeset by Gloucester Typesetting Services
and printed in Great Britain by
Billing & Sons Limited, Worcester.

Contents

Contents

I

Introduction:
Putting Prayer to the Test

1. *'Whatever you pray for ...'*

According to Matthew 21.22, Jesus said to his disciples: 'Whatever you pray for in faith you will receive.' Many believers have some difficulty with the generality of this promise. After all, not *all* prayers are answered, are they? This may have something to do with the condition that they have to be offered 'in faith'. Maybe prayers are often unanswered because they are not accompanied by 'faith' in the required sense. Apart from this difficulty,[1] however, most believers would be willing to claim that God does in fact answer their prayers. Many would add that they know this from personal experience. Even though God does not answer all prayers, or does not always answer prayers in the exact sense in which they were formulated, experience does show that prayers do have effect and are not offered to God in vain.

This claim raises a further question. If the efficacy of prayer can in principle be known from experience, does it not follow that we should be able to conduct an experiment to test the claim that prayers are efficacious? To many the very idea of such an experiment sounds irreligious and even blasphemous. Are we not forbidden to put the Lord our God to the test (Matt. 4.7; Deut. 6.16)? On the other hand, do we not read in the Psalms that 'the Lord's word has stood the test. He is the shield of all who take refuge in him' (Ps. 18.30)? And does the Bible not provide us with numerous examples of people who did put the Lord to the test – and with success? Is not the contest between Elijah and the prophets of Baal a case in point? Did not Elijah conduct a successful experiment on Mount Carmel to prove to the prophets of Baal that the God of Israel answers the prayers of those who call upon him?

To these questions one might reply that the test spoken of in Psalm 18.30 should not be interpreted as an experimental test, and that what Elijah did on Mount Carmel should also not be confused with experimenting. Both Elijah and the Psalmist were *trusting* the Lord and finding that their trust was not in vain. This is something quite different from testing an experimental hypothesis. It would be a category mistake to interpret the believer's claim that God answers prayer as an experimental hypothesis.

But how, then, do these differ? We could learn much about the logic of the believer's claim by asking how it differs from an experimental hypothesis, or, more concretely, how what Elijah did on Mount Carmel differs from what a scientist does in conducting an experiment. This question will turn out to be a useful point of departure for our inquiry into what we do when we pray. In persuing it we could at the same time introduce, in a provisional way, the various issues to be discussed in the rest of the book.

2. *Prayer and experiment: Elijah and Einstein*

Scientific experiments serve to test theories. A scientific theory is a generalization from which predictions can be derived, such that, if these predictions come true, the theory is confirmed, and if they do not, the theory would be falsified. A good example to illustrate this point is Einstein's theory of gravitation which Karl Popper describes as follows:

> Einstein's gravitational theory had led to the result that light must be attracted by heavy bodies (such as the sun), precisely as material bodies were attracted. As a consequence it could be calculated that light from a distant fixed star whose apparent position was close to the sun would reach the earth from such a direction that the star would seem to be slightly shifted away from the sun; or, in other words, that stars close to the sun would look as if they had moved a little away from the sun, and from one another. This is a thing which cannot normally be observed since such stars are rendered invisible in daytime by the sun's overwhelming brightness; but during an eclipse it is

possible to take photographs of them. If the same constellation is photographed at night one can measure the distance on the two photographs, and check the predicted effect.[2]

During the eclipse of the sun in 1919 Eddington made the observations described here by Popper, and thus provided the first important confirmation of Einstein's theory.

Do we not have something similar in the case of Elijah and the prophets of Baal as described in I Kings 18? Elijah's opponents believed that the God Baal answers prayers, and on the basis of this belief they called on Baal all day long – but to no avail. Thus their belief in the efficacy of such prayers was falsified. Elijah believed that Yahweh was God and that he would answer the prayers of those who call on him. On the basis of this belief he prayed to Yahweh who answered his prayer by sending fire from heaven. Thus his belief in the God of Abraham was confirmed before the assembled multitude on Mount Carmel.

The similarities between the examples of Einstein and Elijah are enough to explain why the episode on Mount Carmel is sometimes interpreted as an experiment.[3] However, there are at least four significant differences which should not be overlooked.

1. As Popper says, scientific theories and the predictions derived from them have the status of *conjectures*, i.e. hypotheses which are always open to falsification. As such they are adhered to in a more or less provisional or tentative way as long as they have not been falsified. It has often been pointed[4] out that this sort of adherence is completely uncharacteristic for religious belief. Thus Elijah's action on Mount Carmel was the expression of an unshakable trust in Yahweh, which is quite unlike the provisional adherence appropriate to scientific conjectures. 'Elijah is not verifying deductions, he is yielding himself in prayer, and trusting God for some – no matter what – visible answer.'[5] In fact, part of the meaning of the words of Jesus quoted at the beginning of this chapter is that faith like that of Elijah is a necessary condition for prayers to be granted. This implies that an experiment to test the efficacy of prayer must necessarily be a self-defeating operation: in order to be an *experiment* one would have to view the claim that prayer is efficacious as a conjecture which requires no more than tentative adherence, and this would exclude the kind of faith which is a necessary condition for prayer to be efficacious.

2. Scientific theories are generalizations which apply not only to the situation in which the experiment is conducted, but to all similar situations. The prediction derived from the theory must necessarily come true in *all* such situations if the theory is to be maintained. For this reason experiments are always repeatable. In the case of Einstein's theory of gravitation, Eddington's observations of 1919 were repeated at many subsequent solar eclipses, thus confirming the theory anew. Elijah's action on Mount Carmel was not repeatable in the same way. If the prophets of Baal had reacted to Elijah by suggesting that the fire from heaven in that particular case was merely a lucky coincidence, it is doubtful whether Elijah would have repeated the 'experiment' just to make sure that this was not the case!

3. In science every experiment implies a risk for the theory: If the relevant prediction does not come true, the theory is falsified. Popper explains this with reference to the Einstein example: 'The impressive thing about this case is the *risk* involved in a prediction of this kind. If observation shows that the predicted effect is definitely absent, then the theory is simply refuted. The theory is *incompatible with certain possible results of observation* – in fact with results which before Einstein everybody would have expected.'[6] Thus Einstein would have been obliged to give up his theory 'if observation shows that the predicted effect is definitely absent'. He could of course have tried to reinterpret his theory *ad hoc* in such a way that it escapes refutation. Such a procedure, says Popper, is always possible, 'but it rescues the theory from refutation only at the price of destroying, or at least lowering, its scientific status'.[7] Thus, within the scientific context such a 'conventionalist strategem' does not count as a reasonable course to follow.

If on Mount Carmel the fire had failed to come down from heaven – if Elijah's prayer like the prayers of the prophets of Baal had had no effect whatever – would he also have been obliged to give up his belief in Yahweh? Or would it have been *reasonable* for him to exclaim: 'Woe am I for daring to put Yahweh to the test in this way! Being ignored by him is the just reward for my presumption!'?

Petitionary prayer must be offered in faith, but it may not presume upon God. For this reason it is usually expressed in conditional form: God is asked to grant something – but only on condition that he wants to grant what is asked. The obvious example is Jesus' prayer in Gethsemane: 'Father, if it be thy will, take this cup away from me. Yet not my will but thine be done' (Luke 22.42). Even when this condition is not explicitly expressed, it is still implicitly presupposed. If we suppose that this condition was also implicit in Elijah's petition on Mount Carmel, then every risk of falsification is removed. The only claim that would be open to falsification would be the claim that God *invariably* grants whatever we ask of him, as we ask it. Would any believer be prepared to make such a claim? Would Elijah have claimed this? I think it is more likely for a believer to claim that God always responds to our prayers, but not necessarily in the way we ask of him. In this sense Calvin writes that 'although God complies with our request, he does not always give an answer in the very terms of our prayer, but while apparently holding us in suspense, yet in an unknown way, shows that our prayers have not been in vain. . . . God, even when he does not comply with our requests, yet listens and is favourable to our prayers, so that our hope founded on his word is never disappointed.'[8] Since this claim does not risk empirical falsification, it is not open to experimental test.

4. The above three differences between the cases of Einstein and Elijah can all be explained in the light of a fourth difference: Einstein's theory is used for predicting the behaviour of *natural phenomena*, whereas Elijah's action on Mount Carmel was based on his belief in the agency of a *personal* God.

Natural phenomena are governed by causal necessity. Therefore a theory like Einstein's which is intended to explain natural phenomena, entails the claim that under certain circumstances (e.g. when light from a distant star passes a large heavenly body like the sun) certain effects will invariably take place (e.g. the light will be drawn off course by the sun), because under those circumstances such effects are causally *inevitable*. From this it follows that (1) experiments to test a theory like Einstein's should be repeatable (because under similar circumstances similar effects should invariably follow), and that (2) every test involves a risk for the theory (if the expected effects do not take place, they are in fact not inevitable as the theory claims).

Personal agency is not governed by causal necessity in this way, but is always the result of the agent's free choice between alternative courses of action. The alternative possibilities are given and might be explained by causal necessity, but the agent's choice is not causally inevitable. It follows that beliefs about personal agency (like that which Elijah presumably held concerning the agency of Yahweh) do not have the same form as Einstein's theory. Elijah did not believe that under certain circumstances (e.g. when Yahweh is called upon to send fire from heaven) certain actions of a person (e.g. that Yahweh does what he is asked) will be causally inevitable. It will always remain possible for the person in question to act otherwise, since his action remains dependant on his will. For this reason the episode on Mount Carmel is not repeatable in the way that scientific experiments are (the same effects will not *inevitably* follow) and claims like those of Elijah will not run the same risk of falsification as is run by scientific theories.

Because they are governed by causal necessity, impersonal objects like machines can be manipulated. I only have to bring about the sufficient causal conditions (e.g. by putting a coin in the slot) and the required effects follow with causal inevitability. Persons cannot be manipulated in this way, because someone's decision to act cannot be made causally inevitable. I can try to persuade someone to act by asking him or providing him with good reasons, but his decision to act remains up to him.

Success in manipulating an object is a matter of technique. My attitude to the object in question is irrelevant, as long as my technique is effective. Success in winning a person to follow a course of action is not merely a matter of technique. My attitude toward the person in question is highly relevant. In this sense J. R. Lucas argues that

> St Paul's antithesis between justification by faith and justification by works could be rendered in modern terms as the insight that salvation depended on one's attitude and was not a matter of technique. It follows from God's being a person. Because he is a person, we cannot hope that he can be secured by anything less than a whole-hearted approach. A grudging observance of the law of nature is enough to secure domination over nature, but a grudging reception of the sacraments or a prudential observance of some moral law will not win the love of God any more than it will the love of a human being.[9]

What Lucas says about salvation also applies to the answering of

6

prayer: only prayers which are offered 'in faith', or are accompanied by a 'wholehearted approach', can hope to be answered. Praying to a personal God with the tentative or provisional attitude appropriate in an experiment, is self-defeating.

We can conclude, then, that an attempt to test the efficacy of prayer experimentally, presupppposes that prayer is a manipulative technique or a form of magic, that God is not a person but an object of manipulation, and that the relation between God and man is not a personal relation but an impersonal manipulative one.

3. *Prayer and statistical inquiry: Francis Galton*

It is clear that claims about the efficacy of prayers addressed to a personal God cannot be tested experimentally. But this does not imply that they cannot be tested at all. In the social sciences claims about the behaviour of personal agents are tested – even though the nature of these claims and the way in which they are tested are not the same as in physics or astronomy.

Two points are relevant here. In the social sciences it is important to remember that the attitude of the investigator has an effect on the behaviour of the persons investigated. Thus, whether a request is sincere or wholehearted does affect the chances of its being granted. In an inquiry into the efficacy of prayer to a personal God, only sincere or devout prayers should therefore be taken into account. Secondly, since the behaviour of persons is not governed by causal necessity like that of natural phenomena, personal behaviour is not predictable in the same way either. On the other hand, personal behaviour is not completely unpredictable either. Thus, for example, a request is not by itself a sufficient causal condition making it *inevitable* that the person to whom the request is addressed does what is requested. But it does increase the *probability* in a way that could be shown statistically. One could inquire, therefore, whether devout prayers to a personal God would not increase the chances of the events prayed for in a statistically significant way. Would not a *statistical* test of the claim that devout prayers are efficacious avoid the difficulties involved in an *experimental* test?

An example of this approach is the investigation carried out by Sir Francis Galton in 1883. Galton points out that 'it is asserted by some, that men possess the faculty of obtaining results over which they have little or no direct personal control, by means of devout and earnest prayer, while others doubt the truth of this assertion'. According to Galton, this 'appears to be a very suitable topic for statistical inquiry'.[10] He reports a number of such inquiries which he persued in order to test the claim that devout prayers increase the probability of the events prayed for taking place. The following three examples will suffice for our purposes.

First of all, Galton inquired[11] into 'the longevity of persons whose lives are publicly prayed for, and into that of the praying classes generally, for both of which cases statistical facts exist ready at hand. The public prayer for the sovereign of every state, Protestant and Catholic, is and has been in the spirit of our own, "Grant her in health long to live". Now, as a simple matter of fact, has this prayer any efficacy?' From statistics available concerning 'the mean age attained by males of various classes who had survived their 30th year, from 1758 to 1843' Galton concludes that 'the sovereigns are literally the shortest lived of all who have the advantage of affluence. The prayer has therefore no efficacy, unless the very questionable hypothesis be raised, that the conditions of royal life may naturally be yet more fatal, and that their influence is partly, though incompletely, neutralised by the effect of public prayer.'

Secondly, Galton compared[12] the longevity of clergy, lawyers and medical men. Of these the clergy may be considered 'to be a far more prayerful class than either of the other two', because 'it is their profession to pray, and they have the practice of offering morning and evening family prayers in addition to their public devotions. A reference to any of the numerous published collections of family prayers will show that they are full of petitions for temporal benefits.' The statistics show, however, that 'we do not find that the clergy are in any way more long lived in consequence', and that therefore 'the prayers of the clergy for protection against the perils and dangers of the night, for security during the day, and for recovery from sickness, appear to be futile in result'.

A third example[13] is the following. Galton argues that 'if prayerful habits had influence on temporal success, it is very probable, ... that insurance offices, of at least some descriptions would long ago have discovered and made allowance for it'.

However, 'insurance offices, so wakeful to sanatory influences, absolutely ignore prayer as one of them'. This also applies to insurance offices run by religious believers, which prompts Galton to make the following comment: 'How is it possible to explain why Quakers, who are most devout and most shrewd men of business, have ignored these considerations, except on the ground that they do not really believe in what they and others freely assert about the efficacy of prayer?'

Galton concludes[14] the report of his findings by pointing out that 'many items of ancient faith have been successively abandoned by the Christian world to the domain of recognized superstition . . . The civilized world has already yielded an enormous amount of honest conviction to the inexorable requirements of solid fact; and it seems to me clear that all belief in the efficacy of prayer, in the sense in which I have been considering it, must be yielded also.'

There are various ways in which one might respond to Galton's conclusions. One possible response would be to question his method of statistical inquiry. Thus one might point out that he bases his statistical generalizations on far too small a number of cases. For example, he bases his claim that prayers for sovereigns are futile, on statistics about the longevity of only ninety-seven members of royal houses between 1758 and 1843! He also too easily rejects the counter-argument that 'the condition of royal life may naturally be yet more fatal' but for the effects of public prayer.[15] Would it not be plausible to suggest that during the period investigated by Galton medical care was a hazard to life rather than a means to longevity, and that royalty was subjected to this hazard more than anyone else? This suggestion illustrates the point made by Peter Baelz in his comment on Galton, that it is not so easy 'to isolate the element of prayer from all other relevant aspects of the total situation and so set up a properly controlled experiment in which the variation of other factors is immaterial to the results'.[16]

This response to Galton does not question the supposition that the efficacy of prayer can in principle be tested statistically – even though the way Galton sets about testing it is not satisfactory.[17] Another way of responding to Galton would be to claim that this supposition is a category mistake. It would be meaningful to test statistically whether a specific kind of medical treatment increases the chances that a patient will recover. But is intercessory prayer for the patient a factor *of the same logical type* as medical treatment with regard to the chances of recovery? And if this is not so, is it then so surprising that Galton could not find any instance 'in which papers read before statistical societies have recognized the agency of prayer either on disease or on anything else', or that 'insurance offices, so wakeful to sanatory influences, absolutely ignore prayer as one of them'?[18]

This response to Galton merely replaces one difficulty with another. If one were to claim that petitionary prayer does affect the way things go in the world, but not in a sense which is open to statistical inquiry, the question can then be raised: in what sense *does* it then affect the way things go in the world? Similarly, if we were to say that God does respond to our prayers, but not in the same sense as we respond to the requests of other people, the question remains: in what sense does the believer claim that God responds to his requests? Do semantic moves like these not merely divest words like 'request', 'response', etc. of any meaning they could have for us?

There is a third possible way of responding to Galton. One might grant him that prayer does not affect the way things go in the world, and that therefore all his attempts to find statistically significant ways in which it does, must necessarily produce negative results. But even though prayer does not affect the way things go in the world, it does affect the person who prays. Galton's inquiry reaches negative results because he is looking for the wrong sort of effects. What shall we say of this?

4. *Prayer and spiritual strength: Alister Hardy*

How does prayer affect the person who prays? This could happen in two ways. First of all, even if prayer does not affect the way things go in the world, it does affect the attitude of the person who prays toward the way things go. In this sense Ceslaus Veleck claims that 'in so far as prayer affects anything at all, it affects ourselves, not God. We do not pray to sway God. We pray in order to change and to dispose ourselves so as to receive properly what God has willed to give to us.'[19] Secondly, through this change in attitude the person who prays becomes better able to cope with the way things go in the world. In this way one might experience, through prayer, an increase of spiritual strength or grace in the face of adversity.

According to Sir Alister Hardy we can put the claim that prayer is a source of spiritual strength to the test.

I believe our religion itself should be a dynamic faith – an experimental faith – a faith in the receiving of Grace in answer to prayer. Let us experiment and see. I don't mean selfish prayer for one's own safety or betterment or prayers to alter physical events, like praying for rain, but prayers to have help in our actions. Somehow, in some extraordinary way, I do believe that there is a vast store of wisdom and spiritual strength that we can tap in this way – something which is of the utmost importance to mankind.[20]

Three points should be noted about this view on the efficacy of prayer. First of all, most Christians would agree that even if prayer does not result in changing the course of events, it is often answered by the person who prays receiving grace in order to cope with the way things go. Thus, for example, Jesus' prayer in Gethsemane was not answered by his being spared the passion which was to follow. But it nevertheless resulted in his receiving spiritual strength to undergo the passion. The cup was not taken from him, but he received grace in order to drink it.

Secondly, the remarks made in chapter 1, section 2 on prayer and experiment apply also to Hardy's invitation to 'experiment and see'. Faith in the efficacy of prayer is a necessary condition for receiving spiritual strength through prayer. If one were to adopt the hypothetical attitude appropriate in experiment, then it is unlikely that one's prayers will provide any spiritual strength.

Thirdly, and more importantly, the claim that prayer is a source of spiritual strength does not necessarily presuppose the existence of a personal God as the one who gives us this strength in answer to prayer. This kind of efficacy of prayer could also be explained in other ways. Thus we might follow Frederic W. H. Myers who viewed prayer as a means of receiving spiritual energy from a universal spiritual level of reality in which all our minds somehow unconsciously participate. According to Myers[21]

there exists around us a spiritual universe, and that universe is in actual relation with the material. From the spiritual universe comes the energy which maintains the material; the energy which makes the life of each individual spirit. Our spirits are supported by a perpetual indrawal of this energy ... We must endeavor to draw in as much spiritual life as possible, and we must place our minds in any attitude which experience shows to be favorable to such indrawal. *Prayer* is the general name for that attitude of open and earnest expectancy. If we then ask to *whom* to pray, the answer (strangely enough) must be that *that* does not much matter. The prayer is not indeed a purely subjective thing; – it means a real increase in intensity and absorption of spiritual power or grace ... To say that *God* hears us is merely to restate the first principle – that grace flows in from the infinite spiritual world.

It is doubtful whether this explanation would be any more acceptable to the sceptic than the view that a personal God answers prayer. 'A critic might say that this explanation of "how petitionary prayer works" is almost as puzzling as the theory of *ad hoc* divine interventions which claims that God "answers" prayers by performing a minor miracle at our request.'[22] Nevertheless, the sceptic who accepts neither the existence of a personal God nor that of an impersonal collective unconscious, need not therefore reject the claim that prayer is a source of spiritual power. He could still explain this as the psychological effect of the activity of prayer as such.

We can conclude, therefore, that the view that prayer is efficacious in causing the person who prays to adopt an appropriate attitude toward the course of events in the world, or to be spiritually strengthened in order to cope with events, does not necessarily presuppose the existence or agency of a personal God. Or does it not? In chapter 2 we shall return to this view of prayer as a sort of therapeutic activity and see what difficulties it has to overcome.

5. *The issues*

This discussion of the various ways in which one might try to test the efficacy of prayer, has raised more questions than it has answered. That was what it was intended to do. In this way the main issues to be discussed in subsequent chapters have been introduced in a provisional way. Briefly, these are the following:

Introduction: Putting Prayer to the Test

1. To what extent is it an adequate account of the nature of prayer to interpret it as a kind of meditative therapy which the person who prays performs on himself? If prayer is efficacious, are its effects limited to the psychological effects which it has on the person who prays? These questions will be dealt with in chapter 2.

2. Is it more satisfactory to interpret prayer as a way of persuading God to bring about states of affairs which he would not have brought about if he had not been asked? Are prayers, then, petitions for things to happen? Or does this view presuppose a too anthropomorphic view of God and of his way of responding to our prayers? How does asking God differ from asking other people, on account of the fact that God is not like other people? These problems will be discussed in chapters 3–5.

3. Not all forms of prayer are aimed at bringing about some 'result'. Thus the question of efficacy which can be raised concerning petitionary prayer, does not apply to prayers of penitence, thanksgiving or praise. These are equally important forms of prayer which should also be taken into account if we want to understand the complex nature of what we do when we pray. Attempts to limit prayer to petition or to interpret petition as the one and only key to the understanding of prayer, are onesided and misleading.[23] What then is the nature of penitence, thanksgiving and praise and how are these related to petition? What light does this comparison throw on the nature of petition and on the dilemma that petition must be *either* a way of influencing God *or* of affecting the person who prays? How do penitence, thanksgiving and praise directed to God differ from the same activities when directed to other people? These issues will be discussed in chapter 6.

4. One way of characterizing the Christian way of life would be to call it a life before God – *coram Deo*. In the light of this, prayer might also be interpreted as an exercise in which the believer is trained in living his life *coram Deo* – or, in the words of Calvin, as 'a perpetual exercise of faith'.[24] How does this interpretation of prayer deal with the problems raised in chapters 2–5 concerning the view that prayer is either a form of self-therapy or a way of persuading God? And how does this interpretation of prayer account for other forms of praying besides petition? Finally, how does this view relate prayer to morality and the Christian

13

life? What could it make of Ian Ramsey's suggestion that 'a time of prayer can be like the Christian life in miniature'[25]? These issues will be discussed in chapter 7.

5. A further issue which will return in every chapter, but which is important enough to be mentioned separately, is the following: Prayer obviously has to do with the relation between God and man. The view we take of this relation is therefore constitutive for the way we interpret prayer. Thus, for example, we would adopt quite different views on prayer, depending on whether we take the relation between God and man to be a personal or an impersonal (causal) relation. We have pointed out above that a 'magical' view of prayer presupposes that God is an object of magical manipulation by man, and is as such not treated as a person. The relation between God and man would then be causal and not personal. This would also be the case if man were an object of divine manipulation in stead of a person – a view which would follow from a determinist interpretation of God's omnipotence. In a view like this prayer could be no more than a way in which the one who prays comes to accept the inevitable course of events which follow from God's eternal predetermination.

If on the other hand we interpret the relation between God and man as a personal relation, then we presuppose that both God and man are persons in the relation. The problem is then how this personal relation should be interpreted. Some views tend to interpret this relation as analogous to a legal agreement in which two persons accept certain rights and duties toward each other. Thus in an agreement between an employer and an employee, the employer accepts the *duty* to pay the employee a wage in exchange for a *right* to the work which the employee has to do for him, whereas the employee is given a *right* to receive wages in exchange for the *duty* to do some work for the employer. If the relation between God and man were analogous to this kind of legal agreement, then prayer would not be a way to *force* God by causal magic to do certain things, but it would be a way to *oblige* God to act in accordance with what one takes to be the agreement. Calvin refers to this kind of view of prayer when he writes:

Many have a practice of formally bargaining with God on certain conditions, and, as if he were the servant of their lusts,

14

binding him to certain stipulations; with which if he do not immediately comply, they are indignant and fretful, murmur, complain, and make a noise.[26]

Persons usually enter such agreements with a view to the advantage each party can gain for himself. This is what typically distinguishes such relations from a relation of mutual love or agapeistic fellowship in which each partner chooses to serve the interests of the other and not primarily his own. Or rather, he identifies himself with his partner by treating his partners interests as his own. In serving these interests as his own, he loves his partner as himself. To what extent would this kind of fellowship between human persons be a more adequate conceptual model for understanding the relation between God and man, and hence also for our interpretation of prayer?

The distinction between personal and impersonal relations will be especially important in chapters 3–5, where we will inquire after the nature of petitionary prayer, whereas the distinction between the different kinds of personal relations will be important in chapter 6 when we deal with prayers of penitence, thanksgiving and praise.

Before we come to that, however, we must first find out whether it would not be satisfactory to interpret prayer as a form of therapeutic meditation, and if not, why not. To this we shall now turn.

2

Therapeutic Meditation

1. *Prayer as therapeutic meditation*

Whatever view we take on the nature of prayer, we cannot deny that prayer does affect the person who prays. Some would not only consider this effect to be beneficial, but would also claim that the primary purpose of prayer is to bring it about. On this view prayer can be characterized as a therapeutic meditation which the person who prays conducts with himself. As such it could also be practised by sceptics who do not believe in the existence of a God to whom they have to address their prayers. Auguste Comte, who had constructed a system of rational religion without God, nevertheless considered prayer to be one of the elemental functions of human nature and therefore prescribed for his followers two hours of prayer daily![1] The usual objections against this sort of view are that it makes prayer into something quite different from what it is taken to be in a religious context, especially in Christianity, and secondly that this view of prayer is fundamentally incoherent. Before discussing these objections, let us first examine the arguments of two defenders of this sort of view, Immanuel Kant and T. R. Miles.

1. *Immanuel Kant*

In his *Religion within the Limits of Reason alone* Kant distinguishes between two forms of religion: rational faith (*reiner Vernunft-glaube*) and revealed religion as practised in the church (*Kirchen-glaube*). Rational religion is the freely chosen endeavour to fulfil those fundamental moral duties which everyone can know through reason alone. To the requirement of moral endeavour, the church faith adds various 'statutes' which are represented as divinely revealed and have therefore to be accepted on authority even though they cannot be derived from reason. These 'statutes' include rites and ceremonies as well as concrete representations of God and of the means of salvation.

The relation between these two forms of religion is like that between concentric circles. In the centre of all true religion we find the moral endeavour of rational faith. This is the essence of religion. Because of human weakness, however, most people are incapable of sustained effort in fulfilling their rational moral duty. For this reason they need the 'statutes' of church faith as a means to strengthen their moral resolve. Thus the disposition of obedience to all true moral duties is strengthened by representing these as though they were divine commands. Similarly church-going, partaking in the sacraments and prayer are 'useful means for sensuously awakening and sustaining our attention to the true service of God. They base themselves, one and all, upon the intention to further the morally good.' In this context private prayer serves 'firmly to establish this goodness *in ourselves*, and repeatedly to awaken the disposition of goodness in the heart'.[2]

According to Kant, then, prayer should serve as a means to furthering moral religion in man.

> The disposition, accompanying all our actions, to perform these as though they were being executed in the service of God, is the *spirit of prayer* which can, and should, be present in us 'without ceasing'. But to clothe this wish (even though it be but inwardly) in words and formulas can, at best, possess only the value of a means whereby that disposition within us may be repeatedly quickened.[3]

There is, however, an ever-present danger that church faith can degenerate into a fetish faith. This happens when the rites and ceremonies of the church do not serve to instil in us a sense of moral duty, but become an aim in themselves, a way of pleasing God and thus persuading him to create in us that moral virtue which it is our duty to realize ourselves.

Even where the conviction has taken hold that everything in religion depends upon moral goodness, which can arise only from action, the sensuous man still searches for a secret path by which to evade that arduous condition, with the notion, namely, that if only he honours the *custom* (the formality), God will surely accept it in lieu of the act itself.[4]

In this context Kant distinguishes between two kinds of prayer, the one legitimate and useful and the other illegitimate and connected with fetish faith. These two kinds of prayer differ in at least the following three respects. First, true prayer serves as an aid to the moral endeavour of the person who prays, while fetish faith turns prayer into a 'means of grace' which is in fact a substitute for moral endeavour. Secondly, in true prayer 'man seeks but to work upon himself (for the quickening of his disposition by means of the *idea of God*); whereas, in the other, where he declares himself in words, and so outwardly, he tries to work *upon* God'.[5] In line with this we can also understand Kant's suggestion that in real prayer one is 'conversing within and really *with oneself*',[6] even though ostensibly one addresses God. Thirdly, true prayer 'can be offered with perfect sincerity even though the man praying does not presume to be able to affirm that the existence of God is wholly certain', whereas in fetish prayer the person who prays 'supposes this Supreme Being to be present in person, or at least he adopts an attitude (even inwardly) as though he were convinced of His presence.'[7]

Because of the danger that prayer could degenerate into an act of fetish faith, Kant suggests that one should be satisfied with acting in 'the spirit of prayer' (i.e. acting *as though* our duties were divine commands) and as far as possible avoid explicit verbal prayers. In any case, explicit prayer should not be required of everybody. It should only be recommended as a means to moral endeavour for those who stand in need of it, as long as they still need it.

> Rather must one labour to this end through continued clarification and elevation of the moral disposition, in order that this spirit of prayer alone be sufficiently quickened within us and that the letter of it (at least as directed to our own advantage) finally fall away.[8]

In brief, then, Kant distinguishes between prayer as a means of persuading God to bring about certain states of affairs, and prayer as a form of therapeutic meditation in which the person who prays stimulates certain moral dispositions in himself. For moral reasons, Kant rejects the former and defends the legitimacy of the latter.

2. *T. R. Miles*

Like Kant, Miles distinguishes between prayer as a means of persuading God, and prayer as a form of self-therapy. The former (which Miles refers to as 'pseudo-causal prayer-language') is rejected by him as meaningless on logical grounds, while the latter (which he calls 'performatory prayer-language') is acceptable as a meaningful activity.

Miles uses the term 'pseudo-causal prayer-language' to refer to 'the making of *petitions* to God, as a result of which it is hoped that he will arrange the course of nature in accordance with the requests of the person praying'.[9] Examples of such prayers include prayers for recovery from sickness, prayers for rain in times of drought, and prayers for victory in war. Such prayers are based on two suppositions: first, that 'prayers sometimes produce results' and secondly, that 'these results are caused by God'. Only if both these suppositions are true, would prayers like these be meaningful.

The first of these suppositions is an ordinary empirical hypothesis which could be tested in principle by statistical inquiry. In chapter 1, section 3 we suggested that the proposition that prayer produces results might not be a straightforward empirical hypothesis which could be tested statistically, and that, even if we were to interpret it as such, there would still be practical difficulties in carrying out such a test. Miles admits these *practical* difficulties, but nevertheless maintains that such a test remains possible *in principle* and that the proposition that prayer produces results is therefore meaningful.

The second supposition of 'pseudo-causal prayer-language' is not an empirical hypothesis, because it refers to a causal agent who cannot in principle be observed empirically. We could verify empirically whether event x takes place but not whether it is brought about by God (as would be the case with an observable agent bringing about x). Thus the proposition 'God brings about event x' has no more factual content than the proposition 'event x takes place'. *Factually* these two propositions assert the same.

Miles concludes that the claim that God answers prayers must be meaningless if interpreted literally as a statement of fact. Since this claim is fundamental to all 'pseudo-causal prayer-language', such prayer-language should be abandoned.

> Those who believe on empirical grounds that prayers produce results are logically justified in using prayer as a technique for producing these results. But it is no more than a technique. The suggestion that God is, in a literal sense, the cause of the results is to ascribe to God notions that are quite inappropriate.[10]

Although prayer-language becomes meaningless if taken to be pseudo-causal, it can nevertheless be retained as meaningful provided we interpret it in a 'performatory' way. In that case prayer is not viewed as a way of persuading God to influence the way things go in the world. It is rather a way in which the person who prays determines and expresses his attitude toward the way things go. Thus, for example, the prayer, '"Thy will be done" is not a request at all. In using these words (and similar ones) we are committing and dedicating ourselves, not trying to persuade an unknown agency to influence the course of nature.'[11]

Miles argues that not all prayer-language which appears at first glance to be pseudo-causal, needs to be abandoned. It can often be reinterpreted in a performatory way provided we are willing to take it in a non-literal or parabolic sense.

> We need not be troubled if acts of dedication and commitment involve the use of parable-language, provided, of course, that this parable-language is recognized for what it is. One of the parables which plays a central part in Christian thinking is that of human relations. Not only is God thought of as a loving father; the Christian himself is told to *love* God. Addresses to God as a person are not necessarily, therefore, to be excluded, provided we are not just being simple-minded about them. Thus the words 'Thy will be done' – an address to a 'person' who is assumed to have a 'will' – are perfectly justified provided we are not mislead into taking them literally, and provided we regard the parable of human relationships as a good one.[12]

Of course not all prayer-language can be reinterpreted in this way. Many prayers, like those for rain or victory in war, only allow for a pseudo-causal interpretation. Such prayers have to be abandoned as meaningless.

Finally, Miles is careful to point out that his rejection of 'pseudo-causal' prayer-language does not imply a denial of the claim that prayers could have a causal effect on the person who prays. Thus an act of commitment and dedication could cause the person performing it to become more committed or dedicated. The prayer 'Thy will be done' if intended as an expression of acceptance with reference to the course events take, may lead the person who prays in this way to accept what is inevitable and so to find spiritual rest. In ways such as these 'particular acts of "performatory" prayer may sometimes help a person to lead a more adequate kind of life'.[13]

We can conclude, then, that Kant and Miles both reject the view that prayer is a request to God to change the course of events in the world. They do so for different reasons, however. Kant has moral objections to this kind of prayer: it is an attempt at evading our moral duty by persuading God to do what we should do ourselves. The point Kant makes is important, and we shall return to it below in chapters 4 and 5. Miles has logical objections to this kind of prayer: it is based on purported factual claims which have factual content. The problem here is: in terms of what criterion are we to define what we mean by 'factual content'? Miles applies the logical positivist criterion according to which a proposition is said to have factual content if it is in principle capable of empirical verification or falsification. Since 1957 when Miles wrote his chapter on prayer, there has been a growing awareness of the difficulties inherent in this criterion of fact and above all of its inadequacy as a definition of the sense of 'fact' involved in the factual claims made in religious belief. Few would hold today that the factual claims that religious believers make about God and their relation to him could be accounted for in this definition of 'fact'.[14] Irrespective of the definition of 'fact' which we adopt or the account we give of the nature of the 'factual claims' in religion, it remains true that such claims differ from straightforward *empirical* claims. This raises significant problems for the view that prayer is petition to God and for the claim that God answers prayer which is presupposed in this view. In this sense Miles raises an important issue which, along with the moral objections of Kant, will have to be dealt with further on. We will return to this in chapter 4, section 3 and chapter 5, section 2 (Kant), and chapter 5, section 3 and chapter 6, section 3 (Miles).

The views of Miles and Kant resemble each other not only in what they reject, but also in what they defend. We have shown that they both interpret prayer as a way of using parable-language about God (Kant talks of using 'the idea of God') in order to express certain attitudes and, more importantly, to instil these attitudes in ourselves. Let us now examine the usual objections to this sort of view, i.e. that it does not apply to what is usually meant by prayer in the Christian tradition, and that it is incoherent.

2. *Therapeutic meditation and the Christian tradition*

Two points are often made here. It could be argued first, that the attitudes which people like Kant and Miles claim to be expressed or inculcated by means of prayer are not the sort of attitudes which are characteristic for the Christian way of life, and, secondly, that in the Christian tradition prayer is in fact intended as petition (or penitence, thankgiving, praise, etc.) addressed to God and not as a means of expressing or inculcating certain attitudes in the person who prays.

Referring to Miles, Terence Penelhum expresses the first of these objections as follows:

> Miles, who does reject the belief in a divine individual, takes as the paradigm of prayer the sentence 'Thy will be done', interpreting it as some sort of self-directed performative utterance. He regards it as an attempt by means of a linguistic device to induce an attitude of resignation in oneself, perhaps after the manner of ancient Stoicism ... A willingness to submit without prideful complaint to *what happens*, rather than to *what God wills*, is not a Christian state of mind at all, even if what happens is in fact the will of God.[15]

This objection is not quite fair since Miles explicitly states that ' "Thy will be done" requires to be understood as "I hereby acknowledge the need to do according to thy will".'[16] Such prayer is therefore taken by Miles to be an act of *commitment and dedication* and not of *resignation* at all. The same applies to Kant who, far from recommending an attitude of resignation defends prayer as a means of furthering moral endeavour. Although Kant recommends that we look on our moral duties as divine commands and the fulfilment of these duties as the service of God, he does have very specific ideas about the content of these duties which, according to him, can be derived from reason alone, without reference to God. Some would argue, therefore, that the rational duties recommended by Kant are not to be confused with the attitudes and the way of life recommended by the gospel as being well-pleasing to God. This objection does not apply to Miles for whom prayer can be used to express and inculcate different attitudes depending on the kind of parable-language used. Thus prayer in terms of the Christian parable-language could indeed express commitment and dedication to the Christian way of life. Or could it?

Views on prayer like those of Kant and Miles are also said to differ from the Christian tradition because, in the latter, prayer is intended as petition (or penitence, etc.) addressed to God and not as therapeutic meditation in which we express and determine our own attitudes. We should, however, be careful with this objection. A closer look at the writings of classical theologians and at standard liturgical prayers will show that believers are indeed asked to pray in order to *express* their feelings and attitudes toward themselves, their environment, and God, and also in order to *instil* certain attitudes in themselves. In fact, it seems to be essential to the understanding of prayer in the Christian tradition to recognize its use as self-therapy.

The following examples from classical theological treatises will suffice to illustrate this. In his letter to Proba, St Augustine writes that 'God does not need to have our will made known to him – he cannot but know it – but he wishes our desire to be exercised in prayer that we may be able to receive what he is preparing to give.'[17] And also:

> To us therefore, words are necessary, that by them we may be assisted in considering and observing what we ask, not as means by which we expect that God is to be either informed or moved to compliance. When, therefore, we say: 'Hallowed be thy name,' we admonish ourselves to desire that his name, which is always holy, may be also among men esteemed holy, ... When we say: 'Thy kingdom come,' which shall certainly

23

come whether we wish it or not, we do by these words stir up our own desires for that kingdom . . .[18]

Similarly Thomas Aquinas writes that 'we must pray, not in order to inform God of our needs and desires, but in order to remind ourselves that in these matters we need divine assistance'.[19] And also: 'Prayer is not offered to God in order to change his mind, but in order to excite confidence in us. Such confidence is fostered principally by considering God's charity toward us whereby he wills our good.'[20]

According to Calvin, the Lord taught us to pray

> not so much for his sake as for ours . . . It is very much for our interest to be constantly supplicating him: first, that our heart may always be inflamed with a serious and ardent desire of seeking, loving, and serving him . . .; secondly, that no desire, no longing whatever, of which we are ashamed to make him the witness, may enter our minds, while we learn to place all our wishes in his sight, and thus pour out our heart before him; and, lastly, that we may be prepared to receive all his benefits with true gratitude and thanksgiving, while our prayers remind us that they proceed from his hand.[21]

With regard to liturgical prayers, Alhonsaari[22] points out that these often start with a (sometimes fairly long) invocation in which God's or Christ's properties and deeds are described – to the Divinity himself. Thus, for example, the prayer of St John Chrysostom used at the end of morning and evening prayers in the *Book of Common Prayer*, starts as follows:

> Almighty God, who hast given us grace at this time with one accord to make our common supplications unto thee, and dost promise that when two or three are gathered together in thy Name thou wilt grant their requests: . . .

Obviously such invocations are intended to remind the person who prays of God, and to enable him to acknowledge the nature of God. It cannot be intended to inform God about himself!

From these examples it is clear that when Kierkegaard wrote that 'prayer does not change God, but it changes the one who offers it',[23] he was expressing a view on prayer which has deep roots in the classical Christian tradition. Therapeutic meditation with the intention of expressing and determining the attitude of the person who prays is an essential function of prayer. To the extent, therefore, that Kant and Miles are emphasizing this, they are nearer to the Christian tradition than their critics would admit. The problem is, however, whether prayer is not also something more than therapeutic meditation. This we will have to discuss in the following chapters.

3. *The coherence of therapeutic meditation*

Although Kant and Miles do not deviate from the Christian tradition in maintaining that prayer has the function of therapeutic meditation, they do deviate by arguing that this sort of therapeutic meditation can be practised by persons who do not believe that God exists or is active in the world. In this they not only depart from tradition but also fail to give a coherent account of the practice of prayer. Since certain factual beliefs about God are *constitutive* for the practice of prayer, the latter becomes incoherent if these beliefs are denied. R. W. Hepburn explains this point as follows.

> If I say 'The Lord is my strength and shield', and if I am a believer, I may experience feelings of exultation and be confirmed in an attitude of quiet confidence. If, however, I tell myself that the arousal of such feelings and confirming of attitude is *the* function of the sentence, that despite appearances it does not refer to a state of affairs, then the more I reflect on this the less I shall exult and the less appropriate my attitude will seem. For there was no magic in the sentence by virtue of which it mediated feelings and confirmed attitudes: these were *responses* to the kind of Being to whom, I trusted, the sentence referred: and response is possible only so long as that exists to which or to whom the response is made.[24]

The difficulty with views like these follows from the *kind* of feelings and attitudes which are expressed and inculcated, and the kinds of actions to which the believer commits himself in prayer. Thus, for example, the texts quoted in chapter 2, section 2 call upon us to pray in order that we might evoke a desire in ourselves that God's name be esteemed holy by all people and that his kingdom and authority be established; remind ourselves of our dependence on divine assistance; excite our own confidence in God's charity towards us; kindle a desire in ourselves to receive his gifts with gratitude and thanksgiving; acknowledge the nature of God as the one who is present with us when we call upon him; etc. These are all feelings and attitudes which we have toward God (e.g. feelings of dependence or attitudes like love) or toward things, persons or events in virtue of the way they are related to God (e.g. gratitude for things which are taken to be gifts of God). Clearly it would be incoherent for anyone to express such feelings or adopt such attitudes and at the same time to deny that God exists or is related to the world in the relevant ways.

One might try to counter this critique by pointing out that the theory need not account for *all* prayers. After all Kant rejects prayers which are an expression of fetish faith, and Miles rejects all 'pseudo-causal' prayers. Why not add to this list all prayers which inculcate attitudes constituted by metaphysical presuppositions? Many prayers could still be accounted for meaningfully as a technique in which the person who prays, can, by making use of the idea of God (Kant) or parable-language (Miles), evoke in himself some admirable moral attitudes toward the world and other people. Thus Kant could still claim that prayer instils in us obedience to those natural moral duties which can be known through reason without reference to God. Miles could still account for prayers which instil in us 'commitment and dedication' to those moral attitudes and actions which do not presuppose metaphysical beliefs. Furthermore, as H. H. Price points out, a kindhearted and irreligious person might very well commend prayers on behalf of other people as 'a voluntary exercise in well-wishing . . . They may well make *you* into a more benevolent person, and a more effectively benevolent person, just because they get you into the habit of thinking both carefully and kindly about the needs and the troubles of other people.'[25] In such prayers, neither the attitudes evoked nor the ideas or parables employed need presuppose any metaphysical beliefs in the person who prays.

This attempt at answering our criticism is unsatisfactory for two reasons. First of all, by thus reducing the range of actions and attitudes which could be legitimately evoked or expressed in prayer, the problem raised at the beginning of chapter 2, section 2 is raised again – and this time it cannot be avoided: The actions and attitudes which such a theory allows for are not those which are characteristic for the Christian way of life. Some might object that there is no real difference here: This view recommends exactly the same attitudes as the Christian faith, but *describes* them in secular or non-metaphysical terms. How misleading this objection is, is clearly illustrated by Paul Van Buren's attempt at a secular translation of the gospel. According to Van Buren 'thanksgiving may be understood as the expression of the joy of a man who has found a measure of freedom and who sees signs of this freedom in the world about him. Thanksgiving and adoration express his joy and wonder before the fact that the world is and that he is, and that his historical perspective gives him a way of understanding both himself and the world.'[26] This clearly will not do. Thanksgiving to God is not merely joy about life dressed up in the form of a parable!

A second difficulty is the following. Prayer is an appropriate way for *believers* to express and inculcate certain attitudes in themselves, but it cannot be appropriate without belief. Thus, as H. H. Price points out,

> Intellectual honesty forbids him (i.e. the 'kindhearted but irreligious person') to use this psychological technique himself, though he can and does approve warmly of the well-wishing which it facilitates ... Unfortunately petitionary prayer, at any rate in theistic religions, contains wishful believing as well: the belief that there is a Supreme Being, the Lord of All, who loves everyone of us, and the belief, moreover, that he 'hears' and 'answers' our prayers ... Unfortunately these wishful beliefs are an essential part of the psychological technique which these religious persons use in their well-wishing exercises.[27]

In other words, denying the beliefs would make the technique ineffectual, and trying to use the technique while rejecting the beliefs would be intellectually dishonest.

One might go further than this and claim also that prayer could only be effective as a method of therapeutic meditation for an unbeliever, if he were to resort to self-deception.

> If one does not believe that there is a God who wills anything, to recommend that men should behave toward the world as if they did believe this because it is somehow good for them to

27

do so and should reinforce this behaviour by engaging in rituals that used to be followed because men did believe this is to infer from one's theory of religion a rule of conduct which is, at best, a form of deliberate self-deception which would be rendered unsuccessful by the acceptance of the very theory it is based upon.[28]

The conclusions of this chapter can be summarized in the following four points:

1. According to the Christian tradition, therapeutic meditation is an important function of prayer – some would even say the most important function.

2. This sort of therapy can only succeed if the person who prays accepts certain metaphysical beliefs about the existence and nature of God and his agency in the world.

3. Attempts like those of Kant and Miles to 'demythologize'[29] prayer, turn out to be incoherent.

4. Problem: is prayer not more than therapeutic meditation? To this question we must now turn.

3

Praying
for Things to Happen

1. *Impetratory prayer*

There are many things which I could need or desire, but am unable to bring about myself. In such cases I could *ask* someone else to bring them about for me. In asking someone else, however, I acknowledge my dependence on that person for whatever it is I need to be done. In this sense a request is an 'avowal of inadequacy'[1] and an expression of dependence on the person to whom the request is addressed. I could of course express my dependence on someone else without thereby requesting that person to do anything, but I cannot request without expressing dependence. This does not mean that a request is no more than an expression of dependence. Requests do not only have an expressive but also a prescriptive force: in requesting I ask someone to do something. In this sense requests are aimed at persuading the addressee and not merely at expressing the attitude of the petitioner.

This also applies to petitionary prayer, if taken at its face value as a request addressed to God. Here too the 'petitioner not only presents his desire to God . . .; he seeks by every indication and argument to move God to fulfil his wish.'[2] In other words, petitionary prayer is not merely expressive, but also *impetratory*, i.e. aimed at getting things by praying for them. 'Christians who rely on the word of their Master, are confident that some prayer is impetratory: that God gives us some things, not only *as* we wish, but *because* we wish.'[3]

The doctrine that petitionary prayer is impetratory raises vari-

29

ous problems in connection with God's immutability, omniscience and perfect goodness as well as with the nature of his agency in the world. Before discussing these in this and the next two chapters, it is important to note two presuppositions involved in all such impetratory prayer: First, the things prayed for have what Geach calls 'two-way contingency',[4] i.e. it is neither impossible not inevitable that God should bring them about. Secondly, the prayer itself is a necessary but not a sufficient condition for God's doing what is asked. These presuppositions need some further explanation.

1. *Two-way contingency*

Among the presuppositions which are constitutive for all prescriptive speech acts (including requests) is the two-way contingency of whatever is being asked for.[5] On the one hand, it makes no sense for me to ask someone to do something if I do not presuppose that that person is able to do what I ask. It is meaningless to ask for the impossible. In this sense 'ought' presupposes 'can'. On the other hand, it is pointless to ask someone to do what he cannot avoid doing. It is meaningless to ask for the inevitable. In this sense 'ought' presupposes 'can refrain from'. It is clear that this presupposed two-way contingency determines the limits of what could meaingfully be asked.

Do these also apply to asking things of God? Are there things which are either impossible or inevitable for God to do or to bring about, and which it would therefore be meaningless to ask of God? Could there be such limits if God is omnipotent? According to Hebrews 6.13 God cannot swear by one greater than himself. But then, it would be *logically impossible* to swear by one greater than 'that than which nothing greater can be conceived'! Again, according to Hebrews 6.18 God cannot lie. But then, since truthfulness is part of his nature, he would be acting *contrary to his nature* if he were to lie.

In his *Summa Contra Gentiles* II.25 Thomas Aquinas discusses the question: In what sense could we say of an omnipotent God that he is unable to do certain things? The examples analysed by Aquinas could also be divided into two classes: acts which are logically impossible and acts which are contrary to God's nature. We might, accordingly, claim that God is omnipotent in the sense that he is able to do or bring about all things which are (*a*) logically possible and (*b*) not contrary to his nature. It follows that it would be meaningless to ask God to do (or bring about) what is logically impossible or contrary to his nature. Let us take a closer look at these two limitations.

First of all, we could claim that God cannot do or bring about what is logically impossible. This claim was rejected by Descartes[6] on the grounds that God is not subjected to the rules of logic. Descartes is correct to the extent that the rules of logic do not, strictly speaking, determine what God could or could not do or bring about. But then they do not apply to what God *does* (or to what anyone else does), but only to what can be *said* about what God does (or about anything else, for that matter). Logical impossibility applies to what can be said (*de dicto*) and not to what can occur (*de re*). That we cannot ascribe logically impossible (or contradictory) feats to God, is not because of some limitation to God's omnipotence, but because we do not succeed in asserting anything with a contradictory utterance about God (or about anything else). If we say that God does something and at the same time deny that he does it, we fail on balance to *assert* anything at all.[7] Similarly God cannot fulfil a contradictory request, not because of any lack of ability on his part, but because the request is incoherent and therefore fails to *ask* anything of God.[8] This could be illustrated with the examples discussed by Aquinas. First of all, it is incoherent to ask of God that he should bring about something and at the same time not bring it about.[9] Similarly, God cannot be requested to bring about that a state of affairs which was brought about by him in the past, was not brought about.[10] Secondly, it is incoherent to ask that God should bring about things with contradictory properties.[11] Thus, for example, God cannot be asked to make something which is both white and black (=not white), nor someone who is both seeing and blind (=not seeing), nor a human being (=being with a soul) who does not have a soul, nor a triangle (=figure with three angles equalling two right angles) whose angles do not equal two right angles.

The fact that God cannot be asked to do what is logically impossible, entails that his omnipotence includes his ability to self-limitation. Thus by doing *a* (e.g. making something white) he eliminates the possibility that he could do *not-a* (e.g. make the same thing black at the same time). Every choice God (or anyone else) makes entails the elimination of contrary choices, and hence that the person who chooses thereby limits his own options.[12]

The second group of things which an omnipotent God cannot be said to do, are those which are contrary to his nature. Aquinas discusses two kinds of examples: things which God cannot do because of his incorporeality and because of his impeccability (or freedom from sin).

As to God's incorporeality, Aquinas argues as follows.[13] Since God is pure act and has no passive potency (i.e. the ability to undergo things), he is unable to do those things whose possibility entails passive potency, e.g. to have a body and perform bodily activities, to become weary or forgetful, to be overcome or suffer violence, to become angry or sorrowful, and to be subject to (bodily) change and decay. This argument gives rise to three comments. First of all, the Christian tradition is by no means unanimous in denying emotions like anger or sorrow to God. Are these not ascribed to him in the Bible? And would such a denial not suggest an impersonal view of God? Secondly, most of the examples mentioned by Aquinas are not examples of *acts* but of things which can *overcome* someone. Strictly speaking these are not relevant to the question which acts are possible or impossible for God to perform. Only references to bodily activities (like walking, eating or swimming) would be relevant here. Thirdly, one might ask with Geach[14] whether God does not have the ability to become man and in this way do and undergo all the things which Aquinas denies that he can. Did Jesus not have a body, perform bodily activities, become tired and sleepy, suffer violence, etc.? Geach suggests that Aquinas might try to answer this objection by distinguishing between what God does as God and what he does as incarnate man. Apart from the logical difficulties which, as Geach points out, are involved in this distinction, it clearly does not enable us to deny all sense to the claim that God has the ability to perform bodily activities.

More significant for our purposes are those things which God cannot be said to do, on account of his impeccability. The most important thing here is that he cannot do evil in the sense of acting contrary to his own will, which is the ultimate standard of goodness. What sort of *impossibility* is involved here? I have argued elsewhere[15] that this is not a logical impossibility since there is nothing logically incoherent in a request to do what he does not want to do. Nor does God lack the ability to do things contrary to his will. If he were to lack this ability, he would not do what he wills by choice but as a result of the way he is constituted. Then Swinburne would be correct in asserting that 'he always does the good because that is the way he is made'![16] This would make nonsense of all talk of God doing what he *wills*, and would in fact entail an impersonal concept of God. Rather, God does not act contrary to his will because by nature he does not, like human persons, suffer from weakness of will. For this reason there is not the slightest likelihood that he will ever do evil, even though he has the ability. In brief, when we deny that God *can* do evil, we are denying the 'can of relative likelihood' and not the 'can of capacity'.[17]

We can conclude that it would make no sense to request God to do what is logically impossible since such a request would be incoherent and therefore fail to ask anything. Also, it would be futile to ask God to act contrary to his will since there is not the slightest likelihood that he would ever do so.

Since two-way contingency excludes not only what is impossible but also what is inevitable, it would also be meaningless to ask God to do the inevitable. If God *inevitably* does whatever he wills, it would then be as meaningless to ask him to do what he wills as it would be to ask him to act contrary to his will. But does God *inevitably* do whatever he wills? We will have to discuss this in detail in chapter 4. Suffice it at this point to say that if doing what he wills in inevitable for God in the sense that he lacks the *ability* to avoid doing what he wills, then he also lacks the freedom to *choose* to do what he wills. As we have argued above, this would not only make nonsense of all talk of God doing what he *wills*, but would entail an impersonal concept of God.

It is clear that the practice of impetratory prayer presupposes a *personal* God who can freely choose to do certain things even though he has the ability to do otherwise. Only such things have the two-way contingency necessary for them to be the sort of things which could meaningfully be the objects of petition.

2. A second presupposition which is also constitutive for impetratory prayer, is that God does what he is asked *because* he is asked. In this sense the petition itself is a *condition* for God's doing what he is requested. On the one hand, however, it is not a *sufficient* condition making it inevitable for God to comply with

the request. In that case prayer would become a kind of magical technique by which God could be manipulated by us, and we would no longer approach him as a rational agent who acts from free choice. On the other hand, although the petition is not a *cause* which makes God's response inevitable, it is the *reason* for his response: God does what he does *because* he is asked. In this sense the request is a *necessary* condition for God's doing what he is asked. ' "God brought about situation S because of X's prayers" implies "If X had not prayed, or had prayed otherwise, God would not have brought about situation S".'[18]

In the light of this analysis it again becomes clear that the practice of impetratory prayer presupposes a *personal* view of God. Like human persons, God is taken to be a rational agent. But God is also very different from human persons, with the result that various conceptual problems have traditionally been raised in connection with impetratory prayer. These problems have led many to doubt whether petitionary prayer could meaningfully be interpreted as impetratory. Are the expressive and therapeutic functions of petitionary prayer not sufficient to justify this practice in religion? Let us now inquire whether these difficulties are so insurmountable that we should doubt the personal nature of God and the meaningfulness of impetratory prayer. These problems have to do with the various ways in which God differs from human persons: Unlike us, he is immutable (chapter 3, section 2), omniscient (chapter 3, section 3), perfectly good (chapter 4) and a transcendent agent(chapter 5).

2. *Asking an immutable God*

Is impetratory prayer to God meaningful if his will is immutable and he is therefore unable to change his mind? In discussing this question, Thomas Aquinas states the argument against the meaningfulness of impetratory prayer as follows:

> Through prayer the mind of him to whom we pray is changed so that he does what is requested. God's mind, however, is unchangeable and inflexible . . . Therefore it is not fitting that we should pray to God.[19]

One might counter this argument by denying that God's will is absolutely unchangeable in this sense. After all, are not the

34

effects of God's will subject to change and temporal order? And does this not entail that his will is similarly subject to change? If he is the Creator, it is his will that some things should come into being. But this means that at one moment he wills that something does not exist and at a subsequent moment he wills that it does exist. Is this not a change in his will? Does the fact that God performs creative acts in time not in this way contradict the claim that his will is immutable?

Aquinas replies to this argument by distinguishing the effects of God's acts of will from those acts themselves. The fact that the effect of an act of the divine will takes place at time t_1 does not require that God wills it at t_1 or indeed at any other time. God wills *from eternity* that whatever happens should happen at whatever time he willed that it should happen. That God's will is eternal and therefore immutable, does not exclude that the effects of his will should be temporal and subject to change.[20]

In this way the immutability of God's will could be maintained, but at the price of accepting a deterministic view of the universe. All temporal events would be inevitable since their occurrence would be predetermined from eternity by the immutable will of God. In such a universe no events could have the two-way contingency necessary in order to be objects of impetratory petition. In the end we would have to accept the proposition put to Origen by his friend Ambrose:

If all things come to pass by the will of God, and his counsels are fixed, and none of the things he wills can be changed, prayer is vain.[21]

This view would make impetratory prayer meaningless in another way as well. Not only would all events in the world be inevitable and therefore not the sort of things which could meaningfully be objects of petition, but God would not be the sort of being to whom petitions could meaningfully be addressed. If his intentions are immutably fixed from all eternity, he would not be able to *react* to what we do or feel, nor to the petitions we address to him. He could not be said to do things *because* we ask him to do them. In fact an absolutely immutable God would be more like the neo-platonic Absolute than like the personal being the Bible represents him to be, and therefore not the sort of being with whom we could have a personal relationship.

35

But is it necessary to ascribe such an absolute form of immutability to God? Could we not consider him to be immutable in a less absolute sense consistent with his being a person who is able to relate to a universe in which contingent events occur and in which personal agents exist?

An alternative way of defining 'change' and 'changelessness' is suggested by Peter Geach, and called by him the *Cambridge criterion* 'since it keeps on occurring in Cambridge philosophers of the great days, like Russell and McTaggart'.[22] According to this criterion an entity has changed if a predicate which could at one time be truly ascribed to it, cannot at a subsequent time be truly ascribed. Thus if we could truly describe the sky as blue today, but not tomorrow (when it is overcast), then the sky has changed. Geach argues that his criterion is intuitively unsatisfactory because it would also allow for Socrates to have changed by becoming shorter than Theaetetus as the boy grows up, or by becoming posthumously admired by some twentieth-century schoolboy, and for the number 5 to have undergone a change by ceasing to be the number of somebody's children. These changes are not *real changes* in Socrates and in the number 5. They are '*mere*' *Cambridge changes*. However, Geach confesses that he does 'not know of any criterion, let alone a sharp one, that will tell us when we have a *real* change in Socrates and not just a "Cambridge" change'.[23] Without such a criterion we will have to rely on our intuition.

T. P. Smith[24] has suggested a criterion which seems at least to account for Geach's examples. According to Smith the Cambridge criterion is adequate for all changes in non-relational predicates (e.g. the sky is *blue*) but not for changes in relational predicates (e.g. Socrates is *taller than Theaetetus*). The problem is that in the case of changes in relational predicates, the criterion does not enable us to make out which of the two terms in the relation (e.g. Socrates or Theaetetus) has really changed and which has undergone a mere Cambridge change. Here we still have to rely on our intuition.

Armed with this criterion, we could try to define the immutability of God as follows: God is immutable in the sense that (*a*) he cannot change with respect to non-relational predicates and (*b*) he can change with respect to relational predicates, but in that case the change in him is a mere Cambridge change and the real change takes place in whatever he is related to. Thus God can come to be worshipped by St Augustine but then the real change is in St Augustine and not in God.

In the light of this analysis, Geach suggests that no real change is possible in God's knowledge, power or will.

> If God's knowledge is to be changeless, then a pair of premises like 'It was once true to say: God knows that Socrates is sitting down' and 'It is no longer true to say: God knows that Socrates is sitting down' must not imply that God's knowledge has changed. If God's power is to be changeless, then we must not be allowed to infer a change in God's power from the premise that 'God can stop Miss X from losing her virginity' was once true – before she was debauched – and is now true no longer. (I take this example, like the one about God's knowledge, from the *Summa Theologiae*.) . . . Traditional theology explains that the apparent change in God's knowledge or power is really a change in the creature, Socrates or Miss X, not in God.[25]

Similarly, says Geach, if we disallow these inferences, we may equally disallow the inference from 'God was not going to let King Ezechias recover' (as indeed the Prophet Isaiah declared to him) and 'God did let King Ezechias recover' (after the latter had prayed to God), to a change in God's will. Could not the apparent change in God's will be explained away as a change in Ezechias?

The implication of this is that Ezechias' prayer effected a real change only in Ezechias' circumstances and not in the immutable intention of God that 'Ezechias should die if he did not pray, and live if he did pray'. This implication is similar to the view of St Augustine that God 'wishes our desire to be exercised in prayer that we may be able to receive what he is preparing to give'.[26]

The advantage of this interpretation is that it does not entail a deterministic view of the universe. Real changes are possible in the world, and these both have two-way contingency and can result from the free decisions of human persons.

In spite of these advantages, this view is vitiated by two highly questionable presuppositions. The first of these is the supposition that the distinction between relational and non-relational predicates is sharp and clear. Not only is this not the case, but our conceptual intuitions provide us with a very misleading guide in deciding which is which. Since Aristotle we have been infected with the ontological prejudice that there are only two sorts of realities: substances and attributes. This makes it very difficult to account for relations since they fall into neither of these two categories. Consequently we tend to interpret relations as though they were attributes of one of their terms. A classical example of this is the debate between Galileo and the church authorities on the question: Which of the two substances, the earth and the sun, has the attribute of being in motion and which has the attribute of being in rest? The trouble with this is that motion and rest are not attributes but relations: an object moves (or is in rest) only in relation to some other object. How inadequate this way of stating the question is, should be clear to anyone who, while looking out of the window of a train at another train at the precise moment that one of the two trains started to move on its rails, asked himself which of the two trains was *really* in motion. This question is only meaningful if the motion (or rest) of the trains is interpreted *in relation to* the rails, and not in terms of the relation the two trains have to each other – let alone if we were to interpret movement and rest as non-relational predicates which apply to the trains irrespective of their relation to other objects! How pervasive this blindness for relations is, is clear from the fact that even a competent logician like Richard Swinburne, in his discussion of this interpretation of divine immutability, includes 'moves' in his list of examples of non-relational predicates![27] Also T. P. Smith, in his paper discussed above, considers the following as examples of non-relational properties: smells, looks charming, is afraid, can't be helped.[28] Are these indeed non-relational predicates referring to attributes which entities could have irrespective of their relations to other entities?

If the only unproblematic cases of real change (as distinct from 'mere' Cambridge change) are those where the change affects a non-relational predicate, and if it is so unclear which predicates are to count as non-relational, then the whole distinction between real change and 'mere' Cambridge change becomes problematic.

The second doubtful presupposition of this interpretation of divine immutability is that in cases where change takes place in a relational predicate (and there may be a greater proportion of these than our conceptual intuitions will allow us to recognize!) only one of the terms in relation *really* changes. The other changes in a 'mere' Cambridge way. But why should this be so? If two people get married, does this only change one of them 'really' and the other only in a 'mere' Cambridge sense? And is it so obvious that 'God's "becoming" Creator or Lord of a new creature involves a "real" change only in the created world, not in God'?[29] And what about the example of Ezechias discussed above? Is it so clear that Ezechias' prayer only 'really' changed his own circumstances and did not 'really' affect the intentions of God? Of course his prayer did change his own situation and made him 'able to receive what God is preparing to give' (as St Augustine would say). But did it not also determine *which* of God's intentions was to be realized? And was this not a 'real' effect on God's intentions? In fact, if his prayer only affected himself 'really' and had no real effect on God at all, could it still correctly be described as 'impetratory'? More generally, does this view of divine immutability allow for the possibility of impetratory prayer any more than the 'absolute' view of divine immutability does?

These considerations give rise to an important suggestion which we have to explore further in subsequent chapters: is it not misleading to ask whether petitionary prayer is intended to affect God *or* to affect the person who prays – i.e. whether petitionary prayer is a form of impetration *or* a kind of therapeutic meditation? Should we not rather say that all forms of prayer (including petition) affect the *relation* between God and the person who prays and therefore have a *real* effect on both?

One final remark should be made here, in fairness to Geach. I quoted his argument above in his own words in order to show how tentative and unsure he is himself about this solution. In a subsequent paper he is even more doubtful about the possibility of explaining away (apparent) changes in God's knowledge and will as being 'real' changes only in the objects of God's knowledge and will.

> Knowledge and will are, in the old jargon, immanent acts: to know or will is an actuality in the knowing or willing person . . .; to be the object of knowledge or will is not something that 'really' happens to an individual.[30]

In brief, if we are to accept that impetratory prayer is a meaningful activity, it is not sufficient to presuppose a non-deterministic universe in which events can have two-way contingency and personal agents can exist. We also have to presuppose that God is a personal agent who is capable of *real* responses to contingent events and to the free acts which human persons perform, as well as to the requests which they address to him. Geach's interpretation of divine immutability allows for a contingent universe but not for a God who can *really* respond to it.

This does not mean that we have to choose between either abandoning impetratory prayer as meaningless or rejecting the doctrine of divine immutability. In fact, as John Lucas points out:

> The argument from changelessness is totally misconceived. For change, like sameness and difference, is an incomplete concept: we always need to specify with respect to what something has changed, or is the same as or is different from some other thing. God is changeless in some respects – in his goodness and his love and his faithfulness: but he changes in other respects ... Indeed, if God could not change in any respect, he would not be a person at all.[31]

We can conclude that there is nothing incoherent in maintaining on the one hand that God is a person and therefore capable of change in certain respects (e.g. by *really* responding to contingent events and human actions), and yet to hold that he is immutable in certain other respects: We can trust him to remain *faithful* to his character. As we have argued above in chapter 3, section 1, there is never the slightest likelihood that he will ever become fickle or succumb to weakness of will and act out of character. In other words, God is immutable in a *personal* sense. He certainly lacks the kind of mutability which Virgil (in a mood of sexist prejudice) ascribed to women: 'Varium et *mutabile* semper femina' (*Aenead* IV).

Clearly, the belief that God is immutable in this sense, does not entail that impetratory prayer is a meaningless activity. On the contrary, belief in the faithfulness of God is the most important ground for trusting him and laying our desires before him in prayer.

3. *Asking an omniscient God*

God is omniscient and knows everything in the sense that for every proposition p, if p is true then God knows that p, and if God knows that p then p is true. Traditionally this doctrine has given rise to two problems for the practice of petitionary prayer. These follow from the claim that God's omniscience extends both to propositions about the future and to propositions about our present desires and needs. Let us first examine the problem regarding God's knowledge of the future.

1. *A God who knows the future*

This problem was already put to Origen by his friend Ambrose: 'If God foreknows the future, and if this must needs come to pass, prayer is vain.'[32] In the previous section we argued that impetratory prayer would be meaningless in a deterministic universe. This would be the sort of universe we would have if God were infallibly to foreknow every event and every human action. No event could take place differently from the way it in fact does, and no human agent could act differently from the way he in fact does, for that would falsify God's infallible foreknowledge, which would be logically impossible. As Boethius put it: 'If God foresees all things and cannot in anything be mistaken, that, which his Providence sees will happen, must result.'[33]

One of the most popular attempts in the Christian tradition to deal with this problem was that suggested by Boethius himself. This consisted in denying that we could, strictly speaking, attribute *fore*knowledge to God, since that would entail locating God in time at a point prior to whatever it is that he *fore*knows. Boethius argued that we should rather view God as existing *outside* of time from where he can see all moments in the whole course of time from beginning to end simultaneously, like a spectator on a mountain-top seeing all parts of the valley below from end to end simultaneously. Every moment of time is *present* to him and not past or future.

> His knowledge, ... embracing infinite lengths of past and future, views in its own direct comprehension everything as though it were taking place in the present.... Whence providence is more rightly to be understood as a looking forth than a looking forward, because it is set far from low matters and looks forth upon all things as from a lofty mountain-top above all.[34]

In this way God sees all events *when* they occur and not beforehand, and thus their contingency is not excluded. They could occur differently, in which case God would simply see them occurring differently without the danger of any *fore*knowledge being falsified. Similarly the lofty spectator on the mountain-top can see every event as it takes place in the valley below, without thereby excluding the possibility of it taking place differently – and being seen to take place differently.

The basic difficulty with this view is that it describes time in terms of a spatial metaphor, whereas time is not like space. While time is the relation between events which occur one *after* the other, space is the relation between objects which exist *next to* each other. It is a serious category mistake to reduce the former to the latter as happens when *consecutive* events known by God from his point of view 'beyond' time are taken to be related to each other like the objects *next to* each other in the valley as perceived by the lofty spectator on the mountain-top.[35]

The most damaging way in which this analogy breaks down is the following. If the lofty spectator on the mountain should perceive two spatially distinct objects in the valley simultaneously, they do not thereby become the same object. But if God were to experience two moments in time simultaneously, they would have to *be* simultaneous and thus be the same moment! The view that God 'sees' all moments in time simultaneously entails that all time is reduced to one moment. Our experience of temporal succession would then be an illusion. But if there is no real temporal succession there would be no real *change* either, and impetratory prayer for things to happen would become meaningless. In any case, if God is 'beyond' time then he could not be the kind of being who could have a temporal relation with the world and with human persons. He would not be a personal agent who could respond to what happens in the world. In this way, too, impetratory prayer would become meaningless.

Prayer presupposes a God who can have a temporal relation with man and the world. Then God's eternity cannot be interpreted in terms of timelessness as Boethius suggests.[36] God is eternal rather in the sense of having no beginning or end, being God 'from age to age everlasting' (Ps. 90.2). If such a God were always to have infallible knowledge of all future events in history – then it would have to be foreknowledge, and we are back with the problem of determinism.

A more fruitful approach would be to start from the question:

In what sense is it, and in what sense is it not coherent to talk about 'knowing the future'? One of the ways in which God's knowledge of the future has often been represented is in terms of *seeing* the future. Thus Calvin writes that

> when we attribute prescience to God, we mean that all things always were, and ever continue, under his eye; that to his knowledge there is no past or future, but all things are present, and indeed so present, that it is not merely the idea of them that is before him (as those objects are which we retain in our memory), but that he truly sees and contemplates them as actually under his immediate inspection.[37]

This view is misleading in various ways. First of all, perception presupposes that the object perceived is actually present to the perceiver. It is logically impossible to perceive something which does not exist any more or does not yet exist. Talk of seeing the future therefore entails, as Calvin says, that the future must be *present* to God 'as actually under his immediate inspection'. But then, as with Boethius, the future becomes indistinguishable from the present and temporal succession becomes unreal. Secondly, while the present is the realm of the *actual*, the future is the realm of the *potential*. It is therefore incoherent to talk of 'seeing the future', not because the future is actual but somehow hidden from view, but because it is still merely potential and not yet actual at all. Talk of seeing the future mistakenly represents potentialities as though they were hidden actualities. Thirdly, while there can only be one actual world in the present, the future contains various alternative possibilities, any one of which could eventually be actualized. Representing the future as already present, entails reducing the multiplicity of future possibilities to only one present actuality, and this inevitably leads to a deterministic view of events: like the present, the future does not contain alternative possibilities.

God, being omnipotent, could of course have created a deterministic universe, in which case there would have been only *one* possible course future events could take. In that case it would have been coherent to claim that he knows with absolute certainty what course all events will take – since there would be only one. However, we all know from personal experience that this is not the sort of universe which he has in fact created. He has rather created a world with an open future in which various possibilities could be actualized; a world, therefore, where events have two-way contingency and human beings are personal agents who are able freely to decide which of the possibilities presented to them they will realize. Because this is the sort of world God has in fact decided to create, he has limited his own possibilities for knowing beforehand which future potentialities will become actual. As Brian Hebblethwaite explains:

> God's omniscience, like his omnipotence, is self-limited by the nature of what he has made. In each case the limitation is logical, given the actual nature of God's creation. He cannot determine the future precisely without destroying his creature's freedom. He cannot know the future precisely, if his creatures are indeed free. But these limitations are consequent upon God's decision to create such a world.[38]

This does not contradict the claim that God knows everything which it is logically possible to know. But God knows all things as they are, and not as they are not. Thus he knows the future *as future* (and not as present, which it is not). He knows the possible *as possible* (and not as actual, which it is not). He not only knows *all* the possibilities which the future holds, but also the relative probability of each being realized. He knows all our intentions as well as the relative probability that we will realize them and not change our minds. Above all he knows his own intentions which in the end he will most certainly realize, whatever we might decide to do or not to do.

Geach explains the way in which God knows the future as follows, making use of his well-known analogy of the grand chess master.

> I am not denying that God is omniscient about the future; I think God knows the future by *controlling* it. God's knowledge of the future is like man's knowledge of his own intentional actions, not like that of an ideal spectator.... God and man alike play in the great game. But God is the supreme Grand Master who has everything under his control. Some of the players are consciously helping his plan, others are trying to hinder it; whatever the finite players do, God's plan will be executed; though various lines of God's play will answer to

various moves of the finite players. God cannot be surprised or thwarted or cheated or disappointed. God, like some grand master of chess, can carry out his plan even if he has announced it beforehand. 'On that square,' says the Grand Master, 'I will promote my pawn to queen and deliver checkmate to my adversary': and it is even so. No line of play that finite players may think of can force God to improvise: his knowledge of the game already embraces all possible variant lines of play, theirs does not.[39]

Unlike the spectator analogy, this way of explaining God's knowledge of the future allows for a world of free agents and two-way contingency. As such it does not entail that impetratory prayer is a meaningless activity.

2. *A God who knows what we want*

God's omniscience does not only include knowledge of the future, but also knowledge of our present needs and desires. To him 'all hearts are open, all desires known', and from him 'no secrets are hid'. Traditionally this has also raised a problem for petitionary prayer, expressed, for example, by Calvin as follows:

> Some one will say, Does he not know . . . both what our difficulties are, and what is meet for our interest, so that it seems in some measure superfluous to solicit him by our prayers, as if he were winking, or even sleeping, until aroused by the sound of our voice?[40]

One possible answer is that of Aquinas:

> We must pray, not in order to inform God of our needs and desires, but in order to remind ourselves that in these matters we need divine assistance.[41]

The trouble with this answer is that it in fact turns petitionary prayer into therapeutic meditation and leaves no room for it to retain an impetratory function: in petitionary prayer we are not *asking God* to do anything, but *reminding ourselves* of our dependence on God. As such we address our prayers to ourselves and not to God. They are intended to determine our self-understanding rather that influence what God does.

At this point we might return to the suggestion made above in chapter 3, section 2, that it is misleading to interpret petitionary prayer as a means of affecting *either* God *or* the petitioner. We should rather interpret it in relational terms: Prayer affects the relation between God and the petitioner. The latter does not *inform* God of something he does not know. Nor does he (merely) *remind* himself of something he tends to forget. Rather he *acknowledges* his personal dependence on God in a way which enables God to give him what he could not have given without the acknowledgment.

In order to explain this point, we need to say something about the nature of personal relations, since it is only within the context of a personal relation that petitions make sense. As we pointed out in chapter 1, section 5, personal relations should be distinguished from causal relations. In a sense the latter are a-symmetrical: only one partner in the relation can be an agent, while the other is an object of causal manipulation. His agency is not a condition for what is done to him. Personal relations, on the other hand, are symmetrical: whether or not the relation can be established, depends on the agency of both partners. Thus an agreement between two persons can only come about if *both* partners freely decide to enter into the agreement. The same applies to fellowship: A can *offer* his fellowship to B but cannot *cause* B to return it. On the other hand, B cannot return A's fellowship, unless A has *offered* it to him first. In this way personal relations presuppose not only that both partners are personal agents, but that each acknowledges the personal agency of the other as well as his own dependence on the other for establishing the relation.

All requests take place within the context of such personal relations. There are three ways in which I could try to get someone else to fulfil my wishes. I could *force* the other to do what I want. In this way I make the other into an object of my causal manipulation and turn the relation between us into a causal one. I could also *command* the other to do what I want. In that case I do not force the other to do my bidding, but I do *oblige* him to do so, and thereby curtail his freedom in responding. I could also *ask* the other to do what I want. In doing this I renounce the use of constraint toward the other and acknowledge my dependence on the free decision of the other for his response. 'I want to obtain something from him, rather than subject him to something. I accept his being as a centre of activity and responsibility.'[42] This also applies to petitionary prayer: in asking God, the person who prays acknowledges that God is a personal agent, and accepts that he is at the mercy of God's free agency for whatever it is that he asks of God. It is clear that the way in which I try to get someone else to do what I want, depends on the sort of relation I wish to have with the other. In this way petition can only be meaningful within the context of a personal relation.

Similarly, there are different ways in which one person can fulfil the needs or desires of someone else. He could notice what the other needs, and do it without waiting to be asked. But then the relation between them is somehow depersonalized. It becomes similar to the relation between me and the pot-plant on my window-sill which I water whenever I notice it wilting. When I decide when to fulfil the needs of the other without waiting for the other to ask, then the decision of the other is not a condition for my fulfilling what I take to be his need. If, however, I want to fulfil the needs or desires of the other within the context of a personal relation, the request of the other is a necessary condition for me to do so.

God fulfils most of our needs and desires without our having to ask him. If, however, he were to fulfil *all* our needs and desires in this way, we would be like pot-plants on his window-sill and not persons with whom he has a personal relationship. In this sense petitionary prayer in which we acknowledge God's agency and accept our dependence on him, is a necessary condition for God giving us what we need within the context of a personal relation. Without our requests God can *bring about* what we need, but he cannot *give* us anything in a personal sense. 'God does not need to have our will made known to him – he cannot but know it – but he wishes our desire to be exercised in prayer that we may be able to receive what he is preparing to give.'[43]

We can conclude, then, that the fact that God in his omniscience knows what we need without our having to inform him, does not make impetratory prayer meaningless or superfluous. On the contrary, it creates the conditions necessary for God to be able to give us as persons that which we need or desire.

In this chapter we have tried to show that if we are to interpret petitionary prayer as impetratory and not merely as an expression of dependence on God, then we have to presuppose a personal relation between God and man. This in turn entails that God in fact has created a non-deterministic universe in which both God and man are personal agents. Since these presuppositions seem to conflict with the doctrines of God's immutability and omniscience, we are faced by a dilemma which can only be avoided by either denying the impetratory function of prayer or by interpreting the doctrines of divine immutability and omniscience in personal terms so as not to exclude the possibility of personal relations between God and man. We have suggested ways in which these doctrines could be retained without rejecting the view that petitionary prayer is impetratory.

4

Prayer
and the Goodness of God

1. *Asking a God who is perfectly good*

In an illuminating essay Eleonore Stump recently discussed the logical problems involved when petitionary prayer is addressed to a God who is perfectly good. The main issue could briefly be stated as follows:[1]

1. Whatever is requested in a petitionary prayer is or results in a state of affairs the realization of which would make the world either worse or better than it would otherwise be.
2. If it would become worse, a God who is perfectly good would not grant the request.
3. If it would become better, a God who is perfectly good would bring about the state of affairs asked for even if no prayer for its realization had been made.
4. From this it follows that petitionary prayer addressed to a God who is perfectly good, effects no change and is therefore pointless.

One could try to counter this argument by questioning the first premise: Not all petitionary prayers are for states of affairs which would make the world either better or worse. Is it not plausible to suppose that the states of affairs requested in many petitionary prayers are such that on balance it would make no difference to the goodness of the world whether or not God brought them about? In such cases it would not compromise the goodness of

49

God if he were to bring about the state of affairs only if it is prayed for.[2] Hence petitionary prayer would not be pointless in such cases.

This solution is unsatisfactory for two reasons. First of all, it entails an extreme limitation of the range of petitions which could count as meaningful. In fact it could only accommodate petitionary prayers in cases where it would have no effect on the goodness of the world whether the petition is granted or not. The vast majority of petitionary prayers do not fall within this narrow category. Secondly, as Eleonore Stump points out,[3] it is doubtful whether any petition is possible the granting of which would have absolutely no effect on the overall goodness of the world. All things being equal, granting a petition would at least have the effect of making the petitioner happier than he would otherwise have been.

Another way in which this problem has often been answered in the Christian tradition, is that proposed by Thomas Aquinas. According to him:

> Divine providence not only disposes what effects will take place, but also the manner in which they will take place, and which actions will cause them. Human acts are true causes, and therefore men must perform certain actions, not in order to change divine providence, but in order to obtain certain effects in the manner determined by God. What is true of natural causes is true also of prayer, for we do not pray in order to change the decree of divine providence, rather we pray in order to acquire by petitionary prayer what God has determined would be obtained by our prayers.[4]

I take this argument to mean the following: (*a*) From all eternity God has decreed what events will take place as well as through what causes they will be brought about. (*b*) This decree includes that some events will be brought about by prayer. (*c*) It follows that petitionary prayer is meaningful as the (eternally decreed) cause of some (eternally decreed) events in the world.

This solution is unsatisfactory in two ways. First of all, the view that all events, including our petitionary prayers, occur according to eternal divine decree, implies a deterministic universe, and, as we have argued in the previous chapter, this would exclude the impetratory character of petitionary prayers. Secondly, on this view petitionary prayers are not impetratory at all. They are the (eternally decreed) direct causes of the events prayed for and not requests to God to bring these events about. To say that God brings about events *by means of* our prayers is not the same as to say that he brings about events *because of* our prayers. It is clear that this view does not explain impetratory prayer, but turns it into something else.

We could try, however, to amend Aquinas' account so as to eliminate its deterministic implications and allow for petitionary prayer to be impetratory. Thus we could claim that God in his goodness provides for many of our needs without waiting to be asked. In fact human existence would become impossible if God were only to provide for us on condition that we ask him first. However, as we argued in chapter 3, section 3, if God were always to provide for all our needs irrespective of being asked, this would not only make our impetratory prayers meaningless, but it would also reduce us to *objects* of his care rather than persons with whom he seeks a personal relation. For this reason (and here the amended version of Aquinas comes in) God has decreed ('from all eternity') that he will provide in many of our needs as we request and because of (not by means of!) our requests. He has decided to treat us as persons and not provide in all our needs unasked. If, in this way, we presuppose that God wants a personal relation with us, we can explain how his perfect goodness does not make our impetratory prayers superfluous but rather provides us with a ground for confidence in calling upon him. 'If you, then, bad as you are, know how to give your children what is good for them, how much more will your heavenly Father give good things to those who ask him' (Matt. 7.11).

This solution seems adequate – as far as it goes. But it does not go far enough since it can only account for those prayers where someone asks God to provide in his own needs. Problems remain with reference to intercessionary prayers where we ask God to provide in the needs of others. Would God's perfect benevolence not be compromised if he were to withhold his blessings from some people if others fail to intercede for them? Similar difficulties arise with reference to prayers for the coming of God's kingdom. I am told in the Gospel that I should pray to God regularly for the coming of his kingdom on earth. If this prayer is to be intended as impetratory, does this mean that God will fail to let his kingdom come unless I ask him? To these issues we must now turn.

2. *Asking for the kingdom of God*

If God were eventually to realize his kingdom on earth, even if we were not to pray for it, then petitionary prayer for the coming of the kingdom cannot be a necessary condition for it to come. But then praying for the kingdom cannot in any straightforward sense be taken to be an impetratory request for the kingdom to be realized. What do we do, then, when we say the Lord's prayer and ask that his kingdom should come?

According to St Augustine, 'when we say: "Thy kingdom come," which shall certainly come whether we wish it or not, we do by these words stir up our own desires for that kingdom, that it may come to us, and that we may be found worthy to reign in it.'[5] In other words, praying for God's kingdom is not a way to influence God's intentions in order that he might realize his kingdom, but rather a way to induce desire for the kingdom in the petitioner. The trouble with this view is that it seems to make prayer for the kingdom into a monologue which the petitioner conducts with himself with the intention of influencing his own attitude toward the kingdom which he expects. But does this not take us back to Kant and Miles and the interpretation of prayer as therapeutic meditation?

Maybe we should take a closer look at the metaphor of a kingdom and see what it entails. A kingdom is not a natural entity but an institutional state of affairs which determines the relation between a king and his subjects. In this way the kingdom of God could be seen as an institutional relation between God and man. The coming of the kingdom is then not to be seen as the coming into being of an entity but as the establishment of a relation between two entities. This does not affect only one partner in the relation 'really' and the other in a 'mere' Cambridge way. Both God and man are involved in the coming of the kingdom.

On the one hand the relation between a king and his subjects is not symmetrical. The one partner exercises authority whereas the other is subjected to this authority. On the other hand, this relation is a personal one and therefore symmetrical in the sense in which all personal relations are symmetrical. It can only be established if both partners agree: the subjects have to *acknowledge* the authority of the king, and the king has to *accept* authority over his subjects. This is also true of the kingdom of God.

Donald Evans has pointed out[6] that if nobody were to acknowledge God's authority, he would not have any authority to exercise. He may still be able to exercise power over people, and he may still be worthy of authority, but he will not (logically) have any authority to exercise. In this sense the acknowledgment of God's authority is a necessary condition for the coming of his kingdom. Praying for the coming of the kingdom is more than merely stirring up one's own desire for the kingdom to come. It is also an explicit acknowledgment of God's authority, and in this way a necessary condition for the realization of the kingdom.

Of course, submitting to God's authority is more than merely acknowledging it in prayer. It must also be acknowledged in what people do and not merely in what they say. Hence a prayer for the kingdom to come is not merely an acknowledgment of God's authority, but as such also a commitment to live one's life under this authority. As Calvin says:

> This prayer . . . ought to withdraw us from the corruptions of the world which separate us from God, and prevent his kingdom from flourishing within us; secondly, it ought to inflame us with an ardent desire for the mortification of the flesh; and, lastly, it ought to train us to the endurance of the cross; since this is the way in which God would have his kingdom to be advanced.[7]

Praying, as acknowledgment of and commitment to God's authority, is a *necessary* condition for the realization of God's kingdom, but it is not a *sufficient* condition. My acknowledgment of God's authority only applies to me, and does not make anyone else a subject of God's kingdom. But even if all people were to acknowledge God's authority, this, by itself, still would not be sufficient to realize his kingdom. It is also necessary that God should accept authority over people. He has to assume the role of king, otherwise his kingdom cannot come. Praying for the coming of the kingdom cannot force God to accept authority. He is a person and therefore free in what he does. If he accepts authority over us, then that is something *he* decides to do, and for which he is worthy of praise: 'Alleluia! The Lord our God, sovereign over all, has entered on his reign! Exult and shout for joy and do him homage' (Rev. 19.6–7).

There are therefore two necessary conditions for the coming of God's kingdom. As Calvin says, 'such is the nature of the kingdom of God, that while we submit to his righteousness, he makes us partakers of his glory'.[8] We have to submit to his righteousness by acknowledging his authority over us and he has to make us partakers of his glory by assuming authority over us. In praying for the coming of the kingdom, we fulfil the first of these conditions *and* we petition God to fulfil the second. But will God, who is perfectly good, not *automatically* fulfil this second condition so that it is superfluous to ask him? As we argued in chapter 3, section 1 above, his perfect goodness entails that we can *count on* him not to deviate from his character and to remain faithful to his promises. But if he is to be acknowledged as a person, there can be nothing automatic about what he does, and we should not *presume upon* him! Therefore petitionary prayer for the kingdom can still meaningfully be impetratory: by asking him, we acknowledge that his perfect goodness (on which we can count) does not exclude his being a person (upon whose free decision we may not presume).

At this point it might be asked whether a prayer for the coming of the kingdom could not be a request to God to bring about the realization of both these conditions. Cannot we pray to God that he might also bring about in us the acknowledgment of his authority? Two things could be said in response to this. On the one hand, it would be absurd to claim that a prayer in which God's authority is acknowledged is at the same time a request to bring about this acknowledgment. As W. G. Maclagan says, 'What appears as a petition for grace to make the resolution required of us is in fact itself . . . the resolution for which it seeks to ask.'[9] On the other hand, there is a sense in which the believer, who has in prayer subjected himself to God's authority, could *afterwards*, when looking back on what he has done, acknowledge that this subjection was brought about in him by the Spirit of God. The believer would claim that he could significantly thank God for the fact that he has accepted God's authority in his life. However, this is an acknowledgment of the Spirit, and the Spirit works by *inspiration* rather than by force. The Spirit could inspire me to acknowledge God's authority, but cannot cause this acknowledgment in me without turning me into an object of divine manipulation rather than a person. In the end I have to acknowledge God's authority myself. As the priest said, in Rousseau's book *Emile*: 'To ask him to change my will, is to ask him to do what he asks of me.'[10]

We can conclude, therefore, that if we interpret the coming of God's kingdom as the establishment of a personal relation between God and ourselves, then a prayer for the coming of the kingdom is both an acknowledgment of God's authority by the person who prays, and a request to God to assume authority over us according to his promises. The perfect goodness of God, far from making this petition superfluous, provides the petitioner with ground for confidence in asking.

3. *Intercession*

If intercession on behalf of other people is to be interpreted as a request to God to provide in their needs, then we seem to be faced with a dilemma. On the one hand, a God who is perfectly good cannot make his benevolence to someone dependent on the intercession of others. As Helen Oppenheimer writes:

> What is hard to believe in is a God who is supposed to withhold his favour from some apparently worthy person or cause for whom nobody has happened to intercede.[11]

Here we cannot argue, as we did in chapter 4, section 1, that God in this way acknowledges or protects the personality of the person in question by not showing his benevolence unasked. On the other hand, if we were to deny that God makes his benevolence to someone dependent on the intercession of others, what is the point of intercessionary prayer? Can it still be interpreted as impetratory if the prayer itself is in no way a condition for God's doing what he is asked?

Eleonore Stump discusses this dilemma in the light of St Augustine's claim in the *Confessions* that God had brought him to salvation in response to Monica's fervent and continued prayers on behalf of her son. She argues that

> there is intermediate ground between the assertion that Monica's prayers are necessary to Augustine's salvation, which seems to

impugn God's goodness, and the claim that they are altogether without effect, which undercuts petitionary prayer. It is possible, for example, to argue that God would have saved Augustine without Monica's prayers but not in the same amount of time or not by the same process or not with the same effect.[12]

This is hardly a satisfactory solution, since it merely limits but does not remove the difficulty. If the other ways in which God could have saved Augustine (had Monica not interceded) are in any way worse for Augustine, God's benevolence would still be compromised, and if they were just as good, then Monica's prayers would have made a difference – but one which did not really matter.

Another way to deal with this problem would be to admit that intercessionary prayer for others is not intended to persuade God to do more for the persons prayed for than he would in his goodness have done anyway. Nevertheless, intercession remains meaningful since it evokes in the petitioner a sense of responsibility and commitment toward the persons prayed for. Thus, for example, P. A. Bertocci argues that

> The religious person intercedes for those persons and causes he cares about, not so much because he wants God to do more than he believes God is doing, but because in and through the sharing of his concern his total sensitivity to the problems facing God and man is increased; he achieves a new sense of God's concern (and his own responsibility) for the need of others.[13]

The trouble with this view is that it leaves no room for the impetratory character of intercession. Praying for the needs of others becomes an evocation of the attitude of benevolence which the person who prays performs upon himself – in fact, therapeutic meditation instead of a request to God. As H. H. Price points out, even an irreligious person could accept this as a meaningful activity:

> Of course our irreligious but kind-hearted friend does not believe that these thoughtful prayers or prayerful thoughts make any difference at all to the person for whom you are praying. But they may well make *you* into a more benevolent person, and a more effectively benevolent person, just because

they get you into the habit of thinking both carefully and kindly about the needs and the troubles of other people. Moreover, an irreligious person, if he has reason to think that other people are praying for him, can quite consistently be grateful to them for doing so. He rejects their theology, but he can sincerely thank them for their benevolence.[14]

The above two proposed solutions to our present problem, both presuppose that intercessionary prayer is aimed at stimulating *either* God *or* the petitioner himself to action on behalf of someone else. In previous sections we have argued that this dichotomy is misleading, since it does not take into account the relational character of prayer. To this we must now add a further objection: the dichotomy between divine and human action also fails to take into account the *mediate* nature of divine agency. As Thomas Aquinas puts it, God's action is a *primary* cause in the world, and as such his agency takes effect by means of *secondary* causes. Among the most important of these secondary causes through which the primary cause acts, are the actions of human persons. God acts through the actions performed by us. This 'double agency' theory of divine action does raise some specific difficulties with which we shall have to deal in the next chapter; here we shall assume that these difficulties can be answered, and try to see how this theory could help us with the problem about intercession.

If the 'double agency' theory holds, then intercession is a prayer in which the person who prays both asks God to act on behalf of the person or cause for whom he intercedes, *and also* makes himself available as secondary cause through whom God could act in answering the prayer. Intercession is 'co-operation with that transcendent will of God which is none the less immanently at work in and through men's relationships with one another',[15] and therefore involves both God and the petitioner as partners in realizing what is being asked. Bertocci suggests something along these lines when he writes:

The simple fact is that God does not do all that is worth while for every person without the co-operative interest of other human beings. In a very real sense, when we proceed to realize the value-possibilities in things, for ourselves and for others, God is answering prayer. At any rate, we would not be able to realize these values without God's making them possible. On the other hand, without human concern and dedication to the growth of value everywhere, God could not have the satisfaction of knowing that his children were co-operating in the fulfilment of his purposes for all.[16]

This view has some important implications, not only for intercession, but for all petitionary prayer. First of all, this view excludes the possibility that petitionary prayer could be a way of evading our duties and getting God to fulfil them in our place. Kant's objections to what he calls 'fetish prayer' do not apply here, since petition is here aimed at making the petitioner a more effective collaborator in God's action in the world. 'Petitionary prayer could be seen, not as a crude attempt to boost the amount of floating goodwill in the universe, but as a way of entering into God's purposes.'[17] Similarly, the prayer 'Thy will be done' cannot be a passive expression of Stoic resignation before an inevitable fate. It is rather an expression of active co-operation in realizing the will of God.

Secondly, on this view corporate prayer is more effective than individual prayer, not because it brings more pressure to bear on God but because it enlists more people in the realization of God's will. H. H. Farmer argues this point as follows:

> To regard corporate prayer as though it were an addition sum, so that the more people there are praying for anything, the more certain is the result, merely because there are, so to say, more units of prayer-pressure per square inch being exercised, is, of course, shallow and absurd. More people at prayer means more effectiveness in prayer only if it represents an extention and deepening of fellowship, a passing of more personalities out of the lower and sinful status of isolation into the higher and redeemed status of loving co-operation in God for the high ends of his kingdom.[18]

Thirdly, petition for success in one's own enterprises, presupposes that these enterprises are dedicated to God in order that they may be God's enterprises in which we co-operate. 'The Christian must bring all that engages his own daily activity to God, and in so far as he can sincerely relate it to what must ever be his supreme preoccupation, namely the work of God in the world, he is entitled to pray for its success.'[19]

Fourthly, if the will of God is the criterion which determines what we should strive after, then it is also the criterion for determining what we must pray for. If in petitionary prayer the petitioner makes himself available as collaborator in God's purposes, this entails that he will bring his own will in line with God's will. 'The aim of all our petitions must be the alignment of our own will with the will of God.'[20] But then the petitioner can only make himself available in prayer for the realization of those purposes which are in accordance with God's will.

Decision as to what things to pray for, and what not to pray for, must be left to the divinely illuminated insight of the individual as he seeks with all his best powers to serve the will of God in the immediate situation with which he is confronted. ... There must be petitions which God can never grant, inasmuch as to grant them would be to deny his nature and purpose, petitions, therefore, which will inevitably disappear from the reconciled man's prayers as he enters more deeply into the life of fellowship with him.[21]

In this chapter and the previous one we have tried to show how the traditional conceptual problems concerning petitionary prayer addressed to a God who is immutable, omniscient and perfectly good, all presuppose a mistaken dichotomy: petitionary prayer is taken to be aimed at *either* asking God to act *or* changing the petitioner himself. If we rather suppose that petitionary prayer is aimed at affecting the *relation* between God and the petitioner, and also take this relation to be a *personal* one, then petitionary prayer must be aimed at affecting both God and the petitioner. God is asked to act, and the petitioner makes himself available as secondary cause through whom God can act.

But in what sense does God act *in* what people do and *in* what happens in nature? And how are we to know whether any event or human action is one *in* which God is acting? To these questions we must now turn.

5

Prayer
and the Agency of God

1. *Divine agency and natural law*

Impetratory prayer presupposes a God who can act in the world
in answer to prayer. We have argued that God's transcendence
implies that his agency in the world is almost always mediate: He
acts by means of secondary causes. Of course, as Swinburne
correctly points out,[1] not all divine acts could be mediate in this
sense. Creating the universe *ex nihilo* could not have been mediate.
It could not have been performed by means of secondary causes,
since there were by definition no secondary causes available yet.
Apart from this, however, theists have usually claimed that God
acts through natural events which occur according to the laws
of nature, and also in things which are done by human agents.
These two ways in which divine agency is mediated, both present
us with conceptual problems. In this section we will deal with the
issues arising from God's agency in nature, and in the next with
those concerning God's agency through human actions.

Impetratory prayer entails that God does certain things because
we ask him to. This presupposes that God can intervene in the
course of nature in order to bring about events which would not
have occurred but for our prayers. How should we interpret this
kind of intervention?

It might be argued that God in his omnipotence is able to perform miracles in answer to prayer. If these were taken to be
violations of the laws of nature or the order of nature, they would
obviously require specific divine intervention, since otherwise

they would by definition not occur within the normal law-governed course of events in nature. Of course, on this view one would have to abandon the claim that God acts in a mediate way: in performing such miracles he would not be acting by means of the natural order, but contrary to it. He would not be a primary cause acting by means of secondary causes, but a direct causal agent on the same level as all other causal agents in the world.

This view runs into two major difficulties when used to explain the way petitionary prayer is answered. In the first place, even if, for the moment, we were to grant that sense could be made of the notion of the laws of nature being 'violated'[2] (in the way statutory laws could be violated?), such answers to prayer would have to be very rare. On the one hand, events contrary to the natural order in fact very rarely occur. (Anomalies do sometimes occur, but could we ever know with certainty that a specific anomaly is really contrary to the natural order? Could we ever exclude the possibility that further knowledge of the circumstances involved would enable us as yet to explain the anomaly in terms of natural law?) On the other hand, even if we were to grant that such violations of the natural order do in fact occur, they must of necessity be very rare. It would make nonsense of the very notion of a natural order if it were often violated. Thus, if answers to prayer are only possible in the form of miracles which violate the natural order, then very few petitionary prayers would ever be answered.

Secondly, this view cannot account for the vast majority of petitionary prayers. Most petitionary prayers are in fact for ordinary events which are believed to be possible within the natural order. It is rare indeed for someone to pray for a miraculous event contrary to the natural order. Most believers would probably be inclined to stop praying for something if it should become clear that it could only be brought about by a miracle. Thus David stopped praying for the recovery of his child the moment he discovered that the child was already dead (II Sam. 12.15–23).

If God, then, does not normally answer prayers by means of miracles which violate the natural order, what shall we say of the alternative claim that he answers prayers by mediate action within the natural order? Could events which occur according to the laws of nature count as answers to prayer? The difficulty with this alternative is that the notion of mediate action on which it is

61

based, seems to involve a contradiction. Thus it is sometimes argued that it would be contradictory to claim that one and the same event is both the result of natural causes and an answer to prayer. If an event can be fully explained as the result of natural causes (apart from the act of praying as such), then it would have occurred even if it had not been prayed for. But then it could by definition not be an answer to impetratory prayer which presupposes that the event would not have occurred without prayer. If natural causes are a *sufficient* condition for an event to take place, as is presupposed with events which occur according to the laws of nature, then praying for it to occur could not be a *necessary* condition, as is presupposed in impetratory prayer.

We appear then to be faced with a dilemma. Either an event is the result of natural causes – but then it cannot be an answer to prayer. Or it is an answer to prayer – but then it must be the result of divine intervention in violation of the natural order. Both these alternatives seem unacceptable to the believer.

This dilemma is not unavoidable, since it only arises if we are prepared to accept the view that events are necessarily determined in their causes. According to aristotelian physics and astronomy, for example, the movement of the planets are necessarily determined by the astronomical order. It is therefore equally impossible for a planet to deviate from its course as it would be for two and two to make five. This view is sometimes extended to apply to all events. Thus not only the movement of the planets but also tomorrow's weather follows of necessity from the way the natural order has been constituted from the beginning of the solar system. The only difference is that with some events (like the movement of the planets) we can calculate beforehand how they will occur, whereas others (e.g. the weather) we cannot know with certainty. The difference is not in the degree of natural necessity with which they occur, but only in the extent to which we are able to know their antecedent sufficient conditions and hence predict their occurrence.

It is obvious that, if all events are in this way necessarily determined by the natural order, it would be logically impossible for God, without violating this natural order, to answer our prayers by bringing about events which would not have occurred if we had not prayed. It follows that petitionary prayer for non-miraculous events would be meaningless – except for providing

God with an extra reason for not miraculously preventing events which would otherwise have happened in any case.[3] This would be a rather contrived rationale for petitionary prayer!

This view of the natural order suffers from serious difficulties. First of all, it involves a natural determinism which not only excludes the possibility that God could freely perform contingent acts within the natural order, but also all free human agency. For example 'how can I have any freedom of speech if the sound-waves impinging on your ears as I speak are determined in material causes going back to the origins of the solar system and having nothing to do with my thoughts and intentions?'[4]

Furthermore, this view does not only lead to the conceptual difficulties of determinism, but is itself scientifically obsolete.[5] It is a view of the natural order presupposed by the mechanist and determinist theories in science associated with Laplace (1749–1827), according to whom nature was composed of mechanical particles subject to Newton's laws of motion. This theory implied that the state of the universe (including that of all the particles contained in it) at any given moment, contains the sufficient material conditions determining its state at any subsequent moment, and hence that the course of nature is uniquely and rigidly determined. However, Newtonian mechanics has now been shown to be false and is replaced in modern physics by quantum theory according to which the laws of nature are not deterministic but statistical: they do not determine the occurrence of single events but only proportions in large classes of events. This explains why we cannot infallibly predict tomorrow's weather but can make statistical forecasts about probable trends in the weather. The laws of nature enable us to predict events with a greater or lesser degree of probability (the weather with a lesser degree than the movement of the planets), but they do not determine with necessity which events are to occur. Thus even the movements of the planets cannot be predicted with absolute certainty – especially not their movements over very long periods. Our inability to make infallible predictions in science is not due to our ignorance of laws of nature which may after all be fundamentally deterministic. According to quantum theory it is due rather to the fundamental indeterminism of the universe.

This indeterminism does not mean that we cannot talk of *necessary* causal conditions for the occurrence of any event. On the contrary, without movement in the atmosphere, no rain will fall! However, it does entail that the complete set of causal conditions *sufficient* to bring about any event, will always include some conditions which are subject to chance since there are no sufficient conditions to determine them. It follows that no event can be predicted with absolute certainty because there will always be some of the necessary conditions for its occurrence which remain unpredictable in principle.

It is clear that quantum theory can explain the lawlike structure of the universe without denying its *contingent* nature. The fact that the universe is contingent in this way makes it possible for human persons to perform free acts in the world and to bring about contingent changes in what happens. By our actions we cause contingent events by bringing about conditions necessary for them which would otherwise be subject to chance. But if human persons can intervene in the course of nature in this way, why cannot God do so as well? Divine action in the world need therefore not take the form of miraculous intervention in violation of the natural order, any more than human action need do so.

Explaining the occurrence of a specific event consist in showing that it could have been expected because it was highly *probable* that it would happen – not because it happened of *necessity*. There always remain some of the necessary conditions for the event which remain subject to chance and therefore could not be predicted with certainty. It follows that the scientific predictability of an event does not exclude its contingency. Nor does the fact that an event can be explained in terms of natural causes exclude the possibility that it could have resulted from divine agency in answer to prayer.

We can conclude that the view of the natural order implicit in quantum theory, does not exclude a 'double agency' theory of divine action according to which God could perform contingent acts *by means of* the natural order and not in violation of it. Although in this way we can account for the possibility of God's action in nature, can we also account for the possibility of God acting in the agency of human persons?

2. *Divine agency and human freedom*

God acts by means of the natural order in a way analogous to that in which we do. But, as we argued in the previous chapter, he also acts in what we do. Some would go so far as to say that 'the power of God's love takes effect in human history in no other way than through the wills and actions of men in whom that love has come to dwell'.[6] But in what sense can we claim that God acts 'through the wills and actions of men'? If God were to bring about our actions, do we not thereby cease to be the agents of these actions and become rather the tools by means of which God performs *his* actions? If on the other hand a human person were to remain the originator of his own actions (as he must if they are to be ascribed to him), how can these actions then also be ascribed to God as though they were *his*? In brief, does it make sense to ascribe the same action to two different agents?

An agent is the originator of his own actions in the sense that his free decision to perform them is a *necessary* condition for their occurrence. In this way what I *do* differs from what *happens* to me regardless of my decisions. However, an agent's decision is never a *sufficient* condition for his own action. I cannot perform an action merely by deciding to do so. Unless my factual circumstances are such as to enable me to do what I decide, I cannot perform the action. As Sartre would say, my freedom to act is always a *concrete* freedom: I am only free to realize the possibilities given in my concrete situation, and not to do anything whatsoever.[7] The *sufficient* condition for an action being performed therefore consists of the conjunction of the agents decision and the complete set of factual circumstances which make it possible for him to perform the action in question.

Since the decision to act must, of logical necessity, be taken by the agent himself, nobody can bring about the sufficient conditions for the action of someone else. In this sense one person cannot bring about the act of another. However, one person can always bring about some of the necessary conditions for the action, other than the decision of the agent. You could provide me with the means without which I could not perform the action, or the motive without which I will not perform it. But the means and the motive are not sufficient to bring about the action unless I decide to perform it. Thus one person's action can be a *contributary* cause, but not a sufficient cause of the action of someone else.[8]

In the light of this analysis, the double agency theory can be interpreted coherently: God realizes his will through the actions of human agents, by (*a*) arranging their factual circumstances in such a way that they are *enabled* to do what he wills (in the previous section we argued that this is possible without violating the natural order); and (*b*) inspiring them by his Spirit in order that they may be *motivated* to do his will. In this way, however, God does not deny the freedom and responsibility of the human agent through whose action he realizes his will. On the contrary, it is still up to the human agent to do God's will, and if he decides not to (in spite of being enabled and motivated) then God's will is not done. In this way double agency is a matter of co-operation between two agents and not of one agent using the other as a tool.

There is one more important point which must be added. In his brilliant essay on 'Freedom and Grace',[9] J. R. Lucas points out that we normally talk about 'the cause of an event' in two ways. Sometimes we use this expression to mean the *complete* cause of the event, i.e. the complete set of causal conditions which together are sufficient to bring about the event. In the case of actions, the complete cause necessarily includes the decision of the agent, and can consequently never be brought about by somebody else. However, we use the expression in another way as well. We select one of the causal conditions included in the complete cause and call that *the* cause in the sense of the most important or most significant factor in bringing about the effect. The considerations in the light of which we select the most significant factor are complex, and different considerations are relevant in different circumstances. When the event in question is an action, however, we usually select as most important that causal factor to which we ascribe most responsibility, or to which we ascribe praise or blame for what has been done. The important point is that we do not necessarily select the agent's decision as the most important factor. Thus the believer will always give God the credit for his own conversion or spiritual successes: If it were not for the fact that God enabled me and inspired me to do it, I would never have done it. Therefore, to him be all praise and thanksgiving! In thus considering God as '*the* cause' of his own action, the believer does not, of course, deny that he performed it himself and of his own free will!

Believing in human freedom, as a Christian must, he cannot refuse to speak in the first person. I did it: I could have done otherwise, but I chose to do it. But as soon as he has said this, he has said too much, arrogating to himself a credit that is God's, and speaking as though he were of himself sufficient to obtain his own salvation: so he goes on to say at once 'Yet not I, but God in me', and attributes all to the grace of God rather than himself, meaning by the grace of God all those factors which he recognizes as having been at work in his own conversion and pilgrimage, apart from himself.[10]

Lucas also points out that often we not only give one person the credit for what was performed by another, but we even speak of the one as having 'done' what strictly speaking was carried out by others. Thus 'we speak of Solomon's having built the temple, though it is doubtful whether with his own hands he so much as placed one stone upon another. Thus our ordinary way of speaking allows us to talk not only of one person's having caused the actions of another, but of his having done them.'[11]

Interpreted in this way, the doctrine of double agency is quite coherent.[12] There is nothing inconsistent in ascribing to God responsibility for our actions (and even in talking of God as 'doing' our actions), without thereby denying our responsibility and freedom of choice in doing what we do. Inconsistency would result only if we were to select both God and ourselves as 'most important cause' and thus ascribe primary responsibility to both agents.

This interpretation of the double agency theory implies that God chooses to realize his intentions for the world in co-operation with human persons. But does this not make the realization of God's purposes *dependent* on human co-operation, with the result that God has no guarantee that his purposes will be realized in the end? Is David Basinger not right in concluding that the sort of God presupposed in this theory 'possesses only a very general form of control over his created universe'?[13]

Two things could be said in response to this. First of all, we must admit that this theory does imply that God's control over the course of events in the world is limited, and that his freedom to realize his purposes is dependent on the co-operation of man. But this is not a limitation or a dependence which is imposed on God from outside. On the contrary, they are freely chosen by God as the necessary corollaries of the sort of universe he has freely decided to create. If we accept that God is a personal being who has decided to create an orderly universe in which human persons can exist and freely co-operate with him in the realization of his purposes, then we must necessarily also accept that he will not act in ways which seriously violate the natural order and the free agency of human beings. By granting us freedom of will, God makes himself vulnerable to our independent action.

On the other hand, we must not overestimate the human ability to thwart God's intentions, nor underestimate God's ability to respond adequately to whatever we in our sinful defiance might do to oppose the realization of his intentions. God not only knows all future possibilities and probabilities (like Geach's chess Grand Master referred to above in chapter 3, section 3); his creative resources are also infinite so that he is always able to respond creatively to whatever we might decide to do. As Lucas explains, the answer

> lies in the infinitude of God, and his infinite resource. One plan may fail, but there are always others. As fast as we torpedo his best designs for us, he produces out of his agonized reappraisal a second best . . . Whatever the situation, there are some things he would rather have us do than other things; and in so far as we do them, we are fulfilling *a* plan he has for us; in so far as we do not, we shall be bringing about a situation, undesired if not always unforeseen, which will call for new remedies of its own, new remedies which will themselves call once again for our co-operation if they are to be carried out . . . God, being infinite, there is not just one best, which if frustrated we can never hope to recapture or recreate, but an infinity of bests, so that the very loss of one makes possible the achievement of another.[14]

To the extent that we refuse to co-operate with him in realizing one plan, our non co-operation is instrumental in making a new plan possible. Thus, if we refuse to be his *agents*, we become his *instruments*.[15]

We can conclude that it is coherent to claim that God is able to act within the natural order, and through the free actions of human persons, without violating the natural order or our personal agency, and without exhausting his infinite ability to respond adequately to us – even when we fail to give him our co-operation.

This being the case, it is also possible that a specific event or human action within the natural order, could occur as answer to impetratory prayer to God. God answers prayer by bringing about contingent events within the order of nature and by enabling and motivating human agents to realize his intentions.

3. *What counts as an answer to prayer?*

At this point the theory of double agency raises a further problem. If God, as primary cause, acts only by means of secondary causes, then his agency as primary cause can only be discerned in the agency of secondary causes. God's acts are seen only in the effects of natural causes and human actions. That being the case, how can we know whether a particular event is an act of God in answer to prayer and not merely the effect of natural causes or human agency? If what Farrer calls 'the causal joint between omnipotent creativity and free creaturehood'[16] is necessarily inaccessible to our scrutiny, then we do not perceive how *two* events (i.e. the act of God and the natural event) are causally related. We only perceive *one* event (i.e. the natural event) and take this to be the effect of divine agency – although it could also have been taken to be merely the effect of natural causes or human agency. Whether an event is to be taken as the effect of divine providential action, is like the doctrine of providence as such in that it 'cannot simply be read off empirical fact. It is an interpretation of fact in conjunction with a prior belief in the Creator.'[17] But then, considering an event as an answer to prayer is not a matter of perception, but of interpretation with the 'eye of faith'.

This also applies to miraculous acts of God in answer to prayer. We could distinguish here between miraculous events which appear to violate the laws of nature, and so-called 'coincidence miracles'[18] in which two states of affairs, both of which allow for a natural explanation, coincide in a filicitous way. Thus, for example, the engine driver faints, causing the train to stop within inches of the man tied to the railway line, and my friend from Hawaii happens to walk into my room at the very moment I desperately need help which he alone can provide. In such cases we would be inclined to speak of a miracle even though nothing has happened in violation of the order of nature. (Of course, more is required here than merely an unexpected coincidence. It must also contribute to the welfare or salvation of the people involved. Thus we would not speak of a miracle if the train were to stop within inches of the end of the tunnel or if my friend were to walk into my room at the very moment I was washing the dishes!) Although events like these could be interpreted as miracles (in answer to the prayers of the man tied to the rails or to my prayer when I was in need of my friend), they could also be interpreted as the effects of telepathy or as lucky coincidences for which one might thank one's lucky stars if one did not believe in God. Furthermore, extraordinary events which appear to violate the laws of nature, also need not be interpreted as miraculous acts of God. One could merely take them to be extraordinary or inexplicable anomalies, and leave it at that.

It is clear that to see an extraordinary event as a miracle wrought by God, is to interpret it as such in the light of faith. Without faith we cannot experience something as a miracle. Maybe this is why Jesus could not work miracles in Nazareth where people refused to believe in him (Matt. 13.58).[19]

The same applies to subjective experiences of being inspired by the Spirit of God or receiving spiritual power or forgiveness in answer to prayer. Such experiences could be seen as the effects of divine action or as gifts of the Spirit. But they could also be interpreted as the effects of auto-suggestion involved in the activity of praying as such. Here too, it is only in the light of faith that one could interpret such experiences as the work of God. Only with the eye of faith can we look on our experiences in this way.

This does not only apply to acts of God in answer to prayer, but to all acts of God – including revelatory acts in which God makes himself known to us. It is only with the eye of faith that we can interpret an event, a sermon, a book, etc. as a revelation of God.[20]

Should we conclude from this that all talk of God acting or of God answering our prayers is purely subjective? Are answers to prayer 'in the eye of the beholder'? Do we end with a kind of *Gestalt* experience: the same event can be seen in different ways (e.g. as an act of God or as an extraordinary event) in the same way as Wittgenstein's drawing of a 'duck-rabbit' can be seen as the drawing of a duck or as the drawing of a rabbit[21] – the difference being merely a matter of interpretation? If this were the case, petitionary prayer would turn out to be quite a different sort of activity from what it is usually taken to be. It could hardly be interpreted in terms of a *dialogue* with God (i.e. the petitioner asking and God responding), but would rather be a sort of *monologue* in which the petitioner utters a request, and then interprets whatever happens as a reply to his request – even though it could just as well have been interpreted differently.[22]

A number of points have to be made in response to this conclusion. First of all, we cannot deny that all religious experience involves interpretation. The religious believer interprets what is given in terms of his faith. But this is not only true for religious experience. All experience involves interpretation. Experience is never a matter of passive registration of impressions. The person who experiences, necessarily interprets what he experiences in terms of his own conceptual framework.[23] I experience x as y (the sound on the telephone as the voice of my friend, the picture on television as a picture of Mrs Thatcher, the image in the telescope as an image of the moon, etc.).

Secondly, we should distinguish between two kinds of 'experiencing as'.[24] In some cases the object of experience always allows for two (or more) alternative interpretations which are equally valid. This is the case with *Gestalt* experiences. Thus one would not claim of Wittgenstein's duck-rabbit that is is *really* a picture of a duck and that it is false to see it as a picture of a rabbit. Most of our experiences are not of this kind, however. Usually we will not be satisfied to say merely that we *see* x as y, but will go on to claim that x *is* y. I do not merely interpret the sound on the telephone as the voice of my friend. I also claim that this interpretation is true, because it is the voice of my friend. In such cases it is no arbitrary matter which interpretation we give to our experience, while in the *Gestalt* cases it does not really matter which of the possible interpretations we choose.

Religious experience (including experience of an event as an act of God in answer to prayer) differs from *Gestalt* experiences in two ways. First of all, it is not an arbitrary matter how we are to interpret the experience. The believer claims that his interpretation is true, and he will give reasons for his claim derived from the conceptual framework of his faith. His religious tradition determines his view on the nature of God and on the way in which God acts. This provides him with criteria in the light of which he decides how his experiences should be truly interpreted. In this connection Calvin talks of the Bible as being like spectacles through which we can see clearly how God acts in nature.[25]

Secondly, unlike *Gestalt* experiences, religious experience entails a knowledge claim which, like all knowledge claims, is both subjective and objective. On the one hand it is a claim which somebody makes *subjectively*, or, if a number of people concur with the same claim, *intersubjectively*. Although this claim is (inter-) subjective, it is not thereby arbitrary: The person or persons who make the claim can give reasons for it, as we have seen. On the other hand, it is a claim about how things really are, *objectively*. In this way the believer claims that his interpretation of experience in the light of his faith represents things as they really are. In *interpreting* his experience, he *recognizes* what is really the case.

In conclusion we should point out one further important feature of petitionary prayer, which follows from the way in which the believer claims to recognize God's actions in the world. The ability to recognize God's actions by looking at the world through the eyes of faith, requires training, in which petitionary prayer has an important function. Petitioning God entails that the petitioner expects an answer. This expectation causes him to be on the look-out for God's response and in this way sharpens his ability to recognize the answer when it comes.

> When praying, the believer is ... repeatedly making himself see the world in a certain way in which everyday experiences are fitted into what he thinks is the proper reality; he is repeatedly bending his emotional life and his behaviour to conform to this reality.[26]

In this way prayer becomes what John Drury calls 'the school of seeing'.[27] By praying for things to happen, the believer becomes able to recognize the providential action of God.[28]

In chapter 3 we argued that petitionary prayer is intended to influence *God*. It causes God to do things he would not have done had he not been asked. In chapter 4 we argued that petitionary prayer also influences *the person who prays*. He makes himself available to co-operate with God in realizing God's intentions. To this we should now add that petitionary prayer also influences the *world* in which the petitioner exists: this world can now be recognized as the sphere of God's providential action.

> God sends the rain to the just and the unjust: but to the just who has asked for it, it comes as a token of God's goodness, whereas to the unjust who never says 'Please' and never says 'Thank you', it is a mere climatic condition, without significance and without being an occasion for gratitude; and the unjust's life is thereby poorer and drearier.[29]

6

Praying
and Relating to God

1. *Petition and establishing a relation with God*

In chapter 3, section 2 we suggested that all forms of prayer (including petition) affect the relation between God and man, and therefore have a real effect on both. We now have to explore this suggestion further, and see how petitionary prayer is involved in *establishing* a relation with God (chapter 6, section 1), how penitence (and asking forgiveness) are involved in *restoring* a relation with God (chapter 6, section 2), and how thanksgiving and praise are involved in *acknowledging* a relation with God (chapter 6, section 3). Before discussing these issues, however, we need to say something more about the kind of relation which is to be established, restored and acknowledged in prayer, since the view we take on the nature of prayer depends very much on the way we conceive of this relation.

In previous chapters we took it for granted that the kind of relation presupposed in prayer, is a personal one, i.e. a relation between personal agents, which, in the relevant sense explained in chapter 4, section 2, is symmetrical. This is, of course, not the case in all religious traditions. In fact, even within the Christian tradition the relation between God and the person who prays has not invariably been conceived of in personal terms.

In this connection Friedrich Heiler's distinction between mystical and prophetic religion is useful.[1] Although these are basic forms of religious experience and personal piety, Heiler is careful to point out that they rarely occur in pure form. Even

74

when one of these is predominant in a religious tradition, the other is hardly ever completely absent. The same applies to the personal piety of individuals. 'The devotional life of by far the larger number of religious geniuses represents in varying degrees a mixture of the mystical and the prophetic.'[2] Although mystical and prophetic religion are therefore not exclusive *types* of religion, they are basic *tendencies* in all religion and as such can be clearly distinguished. For our present purposes it is important to note three important differences: They differ in the sort of relation sought with God, in the view taken of the God to whom the believer relates, and in the view adopted on the nature and function of prayer.

Heiler defines mysticism as 'that form of intercourse with God in which the world and self are absolutely denied, in which human personality is dissolved, disappears and is absorbed in the infinite unity of the Godhead'.[3] The mystic strives after an ecstatic experience of union with the Divine. 'The barriers between God and man disappear in the ecstatic experience; man vanishes in God, fuses with him in perfect unity. Every contrast, every difference, every dualism, disappears in the mystical experience.'[4] By contrast, prophetic piety seeks a personal fellowship between the believer and God, a relation between an I and a Thou in which both partners remain independent personal agents and neither is absorbed into the other. 'God and man are never mingled . . . Even the childlike trust of Jesus in God His Father remains always a personal fellowship, it never goes as far as a mystical "union".'[5]

This difference is reflected in the way love for God is conceived of in these two forms of piety. In prophetic religion love for God is understood in *relational* terms as a loving fellowship between personal agents. In mysticism love for God is understood in *experiential* terms as an ecstatic experience of union with God. In nuptual mysticism this is interpreted in erotic terms as analogous to an experience of coitus. Hieler quotes the mystic Heinrich Suso addressing God as follows:

> The bedchamber is closed on our intimacy, our love couch is bedecked with flowers. Come, O my beloved! Nothing remains now but for you to take me in the arms of Thy boundless love to let me fall into a blissful sleep.[6]

These two ways of relating to the Divine, entail different views on the nature of the God to whom the worshipper relates. Thus 'the God whom the mystic adores is conceived as absolutely static. The spiritual Reality in which he by contemplation sinks himself, is a static ideal; the object of contemplation can be only an Ultimate, a Final.'[7] If, on the other hand, the relation sought with God is to be a relation of personal fellowship, then the God with whom this fellowship is to be achieved must necessarily be a personal being.

> The essential traits of personality, thinking, willing, feeling, are as vital to the prophetic conception of God as to that of the primitive man. The worshipper is able to pour out the needs of his heart to none but a God with human feelings; none other could comfort and help him; surely not a supernatural, spiritual ideal. God is not the Sole Existent, the Limitless One, the Supreme Good, as in mystic prayer, but the 'Helper in time of need', the 'Hearer of prayer'.[8]

It is clear that the practice of prayer is quite different in both form and purpose within each of these two forms of piety. In mysticism prayer is either part of the *via mystica*, a preliminary step toward achieving ecstatic union with the Divine,[9] or it is an expression of this ecstatic experience, as in the words of Tersteegen: 'I sink myself in Thee, I in Thee, Thou in me.'[10] The latter usually develops into a wordless contemplation of the Divine.

> All mystical prayer, therefore, tends to pass from prayer in words (either spoken aloud or inwardly framed) to wordless prayer, from speech with God to silent contemplation of God. ... This wordless prayer is a *state of prayer*, not an act of prayer.[11]

In prophetic piety, on the other hand, prayer is aimed at a personal relation with God, and is understood as 'a living communion of the religious man with God, conceived as personal and present in experience, a communion which reflects the forms of the social relations of humanity'.[12] This is so different from mystical prayer, that Heiler seems to doubt whether the latter could still strictly be termed 'prayer'.

> This ecstatic union with God can only be called prayer by the use of an inaccurate metaphor. In these cases of ecstasy there is

no such consciousness of the difference between 'I' and 'Thou' as is essential to all prayer.[13]

If, as we shall argue in this chapter, basic forms of prayer like petition, penitence and thanksgiving, all presuppose a personal relation with God, it is clear that within mystic religion they either become impossible or are turned into something very different. In the light of our argument in previous chapters, this is very clear in the case of petition. In pure mysticism petition cannot be interpreted as impetratory. As Heiler points out:

> God is for the mystic the supreme, changeless Reality whom man cannot influence by prayer even if he should pray for the highest moral blessings. The primitive conception of a real influence of man upon God lies at the root of the prophetic belief in the hearing of prayer.[14]

Petition is related to personal relations in another way as well. Not only is a personal relation between God and the petitioner a necessary condition for petitionary prayer, but petition is also a necessary condition for establishing a personal relation, in the sense that no personal relation is possible unless both partners adopt the attitude toward one another which is expressed in petition. Since a personal relation presupposes that both partners in the relation have the status of independent personal agents, I cannot succeed in establishing a personal relation with someone else if I do not both avow my own independent status as a person and acknowledge the personal independence of the other. Thus personal relations are excluded when I try to coerce or manipulate my partner into doing my bidding and thereby fail to acknowledge his independence as an agent, or when I renounce my own personality or my own wishes as is the case in pure mysticism where the mystic sinks his own individuality in a mystical union with the Divine. Thus Heiler points out that 'mysticism rejects not only petition for earthly things but petition in general. Petition is the expression of wish and will; the mystical ideal, on the contrary, is complete absence of wish and will, freedom from desire, and absolute abandon.'[15] A personal relation can be established only if both adopt the attitude of petition and in so doing avoid these two pitfalls. As John Drury explains, this also applies to a personal relation with God:

Asking is different from commanding and threatening on the one hand and submission and resignation on the other ... It is not the sort of rude and crude magic which sensitive people find so offensive. Neither is it the relieving of worried feelings or the instant resignation to the will of another which they, in reaction, prefer.[16]

Or more positively:

When somebody prays he expresses himself and his needs in a free and uninhibited way. The only restraint he acknowledges is that his prayer should allow an equally free and uninhibited answer. He seeks to move the other. He asks God to see and to act, but he leaves to him just how he should see and just how he should act. There is no grovelling. Like the early Christians he makes his plea standing upright on his feet. In this sense he is strong and active. But he does not attempt to control the answer, which rests with God. In this sense he is helpless.[17]

In brief, in petitionary prayer I do not renounce myself or my own desires (as the mystic does in his search for union with the Divine). But I do renounce the use of constraint in getting God to grant my petition, and thereby I acknowledge both God's freedom as a person and my dependence on his free decision for granting whatever I ask of him. This petitionary attitude to God is a necessary condition for establishing a personal relation with God – as in fact it also is for establishing a personal relation with human beings. In the next section we will see that this is also true when we seek to restore a broken relationship with other persons and with God.

2. *Penitence and restoring a relation with God*

What is involved in restoring a broken relationship between persons? That depends on the sort of relationship which has been broken. In chapter 1, section 5 we distinguished between two kinds of relations between persons: mutual love or fellowship and agreements involving rights and duties. We now have to see what is involved in breaking and restoring these two kinds of relations, and how this applies to restoring a broken relationship with God.

Agapeistic fellowship is the sort of relationship which exists between two persons when each identifies himself with the other by treating the other's interests as his own. In serving these interests as his own, he loves the other as himself. Owing to human weakness, we are all too often unable to sustain this sort of agapeistic fellowship consistently. Through selfishness I put my own interests first, and intentionally or unintentionally act in ways which are contrary to your interests and thus cause you injury. Irrespective of whether the injury is serious or trivial, I have marred our relationship and given you grounds for resentment. In being resentful, you endorse the fact that our relationship has been damaged, if not broken.

Such a breach in our relationship can only be healed if you refuse to be resentful, and instead adopt the opposite attitude, i.e. willingness to forgive. You have to consider the breach in our relationship a greater evil than the injury I have caused you, and therefore be willing to continue identifying with me and treating my interests as your own in spite of what I have done to you.

Such forgiveness can only be both real and effective on certain conditions. Thus it can only be *real* if there is something to forgive. It would make no sense to say that you forgive me unless I really caused you injury by failing to seek your interests as my own. In this respect forgiveness should not be confused with condonation. If you were to *condone* my action, you would thereby *deny* that it is an action which caused you injury, and thus also deny that there is anything to forgive. If, on the other hand, you *forgive* me for what I have done, you claim that my action did cause you injury, but that you would rather bear the injury than abandon the fellowship which I have marred by my action. 'The power to forgive is not to be obtained for nothing, it must be bought at a price, it must be paid for with the suffering of him who has been sinned against.'[18] Thus forgiveness costs you something whereas condonation is a denial that there are any costs involved.[19]

Your forgiveness can only be *effective* in restoring our broken fellowship, on condition that I am penitent and express both contrition for damaging our fellowship and the desire that it should be restored. Forgiveness is your willingness to identify with me in spite of what I did. But if I do not through penitence renounce the fact that I have broken our fellowship, your identification would entail acquiescence in the fact that our fellowship is broken, rather than the restoration of it. It follows that my asking your forgiveness *entails* an expression of penitence and a change of heart on my part. The one would be incoherent without the other. 'To ask to be forgiven is in part to acknowledge that the attitude displayed in our actions was such as might properly be resented and in part to repudiate that attitude for the future (or at least for the immediate future); and to forgive is to accept the repudiation and to forswear the resentment.'[20]

Although my penitence is in this sense a *necessary* condition for your forgiveness, it is not a *sufficient* condition. My penitence can neither cause nor earn your forgiveness. Whether you are to identify with me again depends on your freely deciding to do so. It takes two to repair a personal fellowship just as it takes two to establish it in the first place. Forgiveness can only be freely given, and when it is forced or earned it ceases to be forgiveness. The same is true of penance and of my attempts to make good the injury I have caused. These cannot be more than a token of my penitence or an attempt to put into practice my repudiation of what I have done. They can neither bring about nor earn your forgiveness since this remains up to you to decide. Thus I can never *demand* your forgiveness as a right. I can only *ask* it as a favour. In asking your forgiveness (as in asking you anything else) I acknowledge my dependence on your free decision for granting my request. I may hope that you will forgive. I might even count on you to forgive me when I am penitent. But my penitence does not entitle me to your forgiveness and therefore I may not presume upon it.

If I repudiate the damage I have done to our fellowship by confessing myself in the wrong, and express my desire for the restoration of our fellowship by asking your forgiveness; and if you, by forgiving me, show your willingness to identify with me again, then our fellowship will not only be restored, but might also be deepened and strengthened.

We shall be to one another what we were before, save for one important difference. I know now that you are a person who can forgive, that you prefer to have suffered rather than to resent, and that to keep me as a friend, or to avoid becoming my enemy, is more important to you than to maintain your own rights. And you know that I am a person who is not too proud to acknowledge his fault, and that your goodwill is worth more to me than the maintenance of my own cause . . . Forgiveness does not only forestall or remove enmity: it strengthens love.[21]

In chapter 5, section 1 we distinguished agapeistic fellowship from agreements in which two persons assume certain rights and duties in relation to each other. In this sort of relation I could commit myself to do certain things which you need to be done in return for the right to expect certain services from you. The relation breaks down, however, when one partner fails in his duty to provide the service to which the other is entitled, and thereby forfeits his right to whatever the other partner had a duty to do for him in return. Thus if you fail to fulfil your duties to me, my obligation to do something for you in return, is suspended, and the agreement between us breaks down.

Basically there are three ways in which this sort of broken relation between us could be restored. You could, first of all, try as yet to do for me that to which I am entitled, or, if this is no longer possible, you could perform some other equivalent service for me. In this way you would as yet satisfy my rights and in so doing earn anew your right to the services which it was my duty to provide for you under the agreement. Thus the balance of rights and duties between us will be restored. However, you might for some reason or other be unwilling or unable to satisfy my rights. If you cannot or will not give me *satisfaction*, I could restore the balance by *punishing* you, i.e. I could withhold from you the services to which you would have been entitled if you had fulfilled your duties towards me. If you have borne your punishment and paid your penalty, your debt towards me is eliminated and the balance of rights and duties between us is restored. Providing satisfaction and being punished are therefore two ways in which the guilty party could *earn* reinstatement in the relation which he has broken. In this respect satisfaction and punishment should not be confused with penitence and penance which, as we argued above, neither force nor earn reinstatement in fellowship.[22] There is a third way in which a breach in a relation of rights and duties could also be restored: I could decide to *condone* what you have done by waiving my right to the duties which you have failed to fulfil. I decide that the service which you have failed to provide is not important to me and that it would not affect my interests if we were simply to amend the agreement in order to let you off the hook.

In sum, whereas broken fellowship can only be restored by penitence and forgiveness, broken agreements are restored by satisfaction, punishment or condonation. If we do not clearly distinguish agapeistic fellowship from an agreement of rights and duties, we will also tend to confuse penitence with punishment and forgiveness with condonation. We now have to see how these distinctions apply to our understanding of the relation between God and human persons, and of the nature of penitential prayers.

It is clear from the foregoing argument that penitential prayers, in which we confess our sins to God and ask his forgiveness, presuppose that the God to whom we pray is a personal Being with whom we may enter into a personal relationship. If we adopt an impersonal view of God, then similar problems arise with respect to penitential prayers as we have shown in previous chapters to arise with petitionary prayers. Thus Anne C. Minas, who takes such an impersonal view of God, concludes that a divine being 'logically cannot forgive, since possession of divine attributes logically precludes conditions which are necessary for forgiveness. . . . Only a human being can forgive – a divine being cannot'.[23] Furthermore, praying for divine forgiveness is aimed at restoring a relation of agapeistic fellowship with God and not at restoring a balance of rights and duties. If we were to interpret the relation between God and human persons in terms of rights and duties, this would either make prayers for divine forgiveness inappropriate, or turn them into acts which somehow merit the restoration of one's rights before God, or into requests for divine condonation or remission of penalty. Obviously this also has consequences for the way we interpret the doctrine of atonement.[24]

In these respects prayers for divine forgiveness are like asking the forgiveness of other people. However, God is not like other people, and there are at least four important respects in which penitential prayer differs from expressions of penitence towards others.

First of all, as we have pointed out above, your forgiveness depends on your free decision. Since it is in no way necessitated, there are limits to the extent to which I could count on it. Being human, you might find it difficult to forgive and suppress your resentment for the injury I caused you. With God this is different. Because he is *perfect* in love, there is never the slightest likelihood (in the sense explained in chapter 3, section 1) that he will ever fail to forgive those who are truly penitent. 'If we confess our sins, he is just and may be trusted to forgive our sins and cleanse us from every kind of wrong' (I John 1.9). However, this does not contradict the claim that his forgiveness is free and neither merited nor necessitated by our penitence. As Peter Baelz explains:

> The penitent is not only voicing his sincere grief and contrition when he asks for forgiveness; he is also asking for something which he has no moral right to expect. He is asking for a new, undeserved expression of the divine love which will restore him to a right relationship. Although in one sense he may be confident of the unchanging love of God, in another sense that is just what he has no *right* to presume upon. To presume upon love is to blaspheme against it: '*Dieu pardonnera, car c'est son métier*'.[25]

Although I could be infinitely more confident of divine forgiveness than of human forgiveness, both kinds of forgiveness remain equally free and unmerited.

Secondly, when I express my penitence to someone whom I have injured, I inform that person of the fact that I am penitent and desire forgiveness. Without my expression of penitence, the other cannot know that I am penitent and therefore cannot forgive me either. With God this is different, for God knows the secrets of my heart without my having to inform him. As Kierkegaard explains:

> The person making the confession is not like a servant that gives account to his lord for the management which is given over to him because the lord could not manage all or be present in all places. The all-knowing One was present at each instant for which reckoning shall be made in the account . . . Nor is the person confessing like one that confides in a friend to whom sooner or later he reveals things that the friend did not previously know. The all-knowing One does not get to know something about the maker of the confession . . .[26]

Although penitential prayers do not tell God something he

does not already know, they do acknowledge and welcome the fact that he knows it.

> We confess in order to express our acceptance of this fact, our willingness to be so known, and our desire to enter as far as we can into this searching knowledge God has of us. We stop the life of concealment, of pretending that no one knows or need know. We say we know we are living in the light, we are content to have it so, only more so, we want to be wholly in the light if possible.[27]

If divine forgiveness is to be effective in restoring the personal fellowship between God and the penitent, then this *acknowledgment* is a necessary condition for God to forgive. Without such acknowledgment the penitent remains an *object* of God's knowledge but does not become a *person* in relation to God. C. S. Lewis explains this point as follows:

> To be known by God is to be ... in the category of things. We are, like earthworms, cabbages and nebulae, objects of Divine knowledge. But when we (*a*) become aware of the fact – the present fact, not the generalization – and (*b*) assent with all our will to be so known, then we treat ourselves, in relation to God, not as things but as persons. We have unveiled. Not that any veil could have baffled His sight. The change is in us. The passive changes to the active. Instead of merely being known, we show, we tell, we offer ourselves to view ... By unveiling, by confessing our sins and 'making known' our requests, we assume the high rank of persons before Him. And He, descending, becomes a Person to us.[28]

It is therefore not sufficient to say with Kierkegaard that 'not God, but you, the maker of the confession, get to know something by your act of confession'.[29] The maker of the confession does not merely get to *know* something. He also assumes the status of a person and therefore of the sort of being with whom God can restore a personal fellowship.

A third difference between divine and human forgiveness is the following. Since my asking *your* forgiveness is aimed at restoring the fellowship which I marred by injuring *you*, it only makes sense if I ask you to forgive what I did to you and not the injury I do to others or my moral transgressions in general. In fact, your forgiveness does not even cover the injury I do to you completely, for, as W. G. Maclagan points out, 'when . . . injury is considered not as injury but in its character of wickedness or evil-doing we recognize that, so regarded, it is something that no man, not even the person injured, can properly be said to forgive. Men can forgive injuries; they cannot forgive sins.'[30] Thus you can forgive my injuring *your good*, but not the fact that in so doing I outrage *goodness* as such. At this point the parallel between divine and human forgiveness breaks down: Unlike us, God can and does forgive sins. However, it does not break down completely, for, as I have argued elsewhere,[31] a believer is someone who accepts the will of God as *ultimate* standard of goodness. It follows from this that all sin, as outrage against goodness, is for the believer an outrage against the will of God and as such an injury to God in which the loving fellowship with God is marred. For this reason I can ask divine forgiveness for *all* my sins, whereas I can only ask your forgiveness for injury I do to you.

This third difference between divine and human forgiveness, entails a fourth. If I am penitent and you forgive me, my fellowship with you could be restored. But your forgiveness does not restore my fellowship with God which was also marred by the injury I did to you. For this reason, if I am a believer, I would not be satisfied with your forgiveness alone. I would want God's forgiveness as well. Only then would my sin be blotted out completely. Of God alone can it be said that 'as far as the east is from the west, so far does he remove our transgressions from us' (Ps. 103.12). Only if I know that God accepts me, can I come to accept myself. Or stronger: if I know that God accepts me, it would be meaningless for me *not* to accept myself. As D. Z. Phillips explains:

> It makes sense to say, 'My friend forgives me, but I cannot forgive myself', but it makes no sense to say, 'God forgives me, but I cannot forgive myself' . . . Being able to see that one is forgiven by God entails being able to live with oneself.[32]

In brief, penitential prayer enables God to forgive and restore our fellowship with him. The believer will also claim that, since divine forgiveness, unlike human forgiveness, blots out my sins, knowing that I am forgiven by God restores my life to meaningfulness. Through penitential prayer 'one just gets to know oneself and finds that one can live with this self-knowledge in the realm of grace, that is to say, knowing that one is accepted by God and that his presence makes each returning day a thing of hope and joy. This is what Jesus meant by "going down to one's house justified".'[33]

3. Thanksgiving and acknowledging a relation with God

Thanksgiving is an expression of gratitude, and gratitude, like resentment and forgiveness, is what P. F. Strawson calls a 're-active attitude',[34] i.e. an attitude which I adopt toward somebody else in response to his general behaviour, including his intentional actions and attitudes, and especially his actions and attitudes in relation to me. But what sort of reactive attitude is gratitude and how does it differ from the others? When would it make sense for me to be grateful to you, and under what circumstances would gratitude be an incoherent response? We could distinguish at least four necessary conditions for gratitude to be a meaningful response to somebody else.

First of all, I logically can only be grateful to you for what you *do*, and not for what you are or for what happens to you. I could admire you or envy you both for what you do and also for what you are or what happens to you, but my gratitude can only apply to your actions. Furthermore (as we shall try to argue in more detail presently) my gratitude can only apply to what you do *intentionally* and not to unintended or unforeseen or regretted effects of what you do. I could be pleased or displeased about such effects of your actions, but not grateful, since they are not part of what you intended.

Secondly, I logically cannot be grateful to you for everything you do, but only for your actions in as far as they affect me, and are intended to affect me.

> If someone's actions help me to some benefit I desire, then I am benefited in any case; but if he intended them so to benefit me because of his general goodwill towards me, I shall reasonably feel a gratitude which I should not feel at all if the benefit was an incidental consequence, unintended or even regretted by him, of some plan of action with a different aim.[35]

In this respect *thanksgiving* (in which I express my gratitude) differs from *praise* (in which I express my admiration). I can praise you for what you do in general, irrespective of whether your action is intended to affect me. My gratitude, however, applies only to what you do *for me*.

Thirdly, I cannot thank you for anything and everything you do with the intention of affecting me. Gratitude only applies to those actions which affect me *positively* – and are intended by you to affect me positively.

> It is natural to feel grateful for the first paper-rack one receives as a wedding gift, but it is difficult to feel grateful for the fifth! One would have been grateful if the gift had been something other than a paper-rack. Or even if someone said that he was grateful for all gifts, no matter how unfortunate the choice, my point still holds: gratitude is connected with the good intentions of the giver. It would be extremely odd, on the other hand, given that there were no explanatory circumstances, to be grateful to someone for not giving one a gift, or for giving a paper-rack knowing one had four already.[36]

In this respect gratitude differs from resentment and forgiveness. These three reactive attitudes apply only to what you do to me intentionally, but, whereas resentment and forgiveness apply to your actions which are intentionally injurous to me, gratitude apply to your actions which intentionally benefit me. Like praise, thanksgiving is always 'linked to the fact that *this* was done rather than *that*'.[37] I praise you for doing what I approve rather than what I disapprove. If you had done something of which I disapprove, I would have blamed you instead. Similarly, I thank you for doing something which benefits me rather than injuring me. If you had done something to my detriment instead, I would either have resented it or I could have decided to forgive you.

Fourthly, I am only grateful to you for the good things you do for me, on condition that your doing them is a favour and not an obligation. The moment I come to consider what you do for me as something to which I have a right, I shall tend to take your action on my behalf for granted rather than to be grateful to you for doing it. This also applies in cases where I mistakenly think it is something to which I am entitled and which you are therefore obliged to do for me. Alhonsaari explains this point with the following example.

Suppose you give me 500 Marks without reason. The only thing I can do is to thank you sincerely. Next year on exactly the same day you again give me 500 Marks. I am again surprised and I thank you. This happens again in the third year. I begin now to anticipate what will happen in the fourth year and in the fifth year I begin to feel it normal for you to send me this money yearly. If you fail to send the money in the tenth year, I feel disappointed and betrayed. Gradually I was led to think that the money belonged to me and that you in a way had promised it to me. Gradually I had come to think that in giving me money you did not do anything beyond your obligations, but that it was more or less the proper thing for you to do, a thing I could expect of you. But I would be wrong all the time in thinking so.[38]

Thus in thanking you for what you have done for me, I acknowledge that what you have done is a *favour* which you freely bestow on me and not something to which I was entitled. In this way thanksgiving entails the acknowledgment that the relation between us is one of fellowship rather than an agreement of rights and duties where you do things for me in fulfilment of your obligations to me under the agreement. In this respect thanksgiving is like petition since both presuppose a relation of fellowship. In an agreement of rights and duties I can *demand* from you what is my right, but in a relation of fellowship what you do for me is a favour which I can ask but which I cannot demand. Thus petition entails an acknowledgment that what I request from you is a favour which you can freely give rather than a duty which you are obliged to fulfil. Thanksgiving entails the same acknowledgment with reference to what you have done for me.

In most respects thanking (and praising) God is like thanking (and praising) other people. I thank (and praise) God for what he *does* and thereby acknowledge that he is a personal agent. In praising God I acknowledge that what he does is good, and in thanking him I acknowledge that it is to my advantage – and intended by him to be to my advantage. Also, in thanking him I acknowledge that the relation between us is one of fellowship: what he does for me is a favour (or grace freely bestowed) and not something to which I am entitled. Thus all three basic forms of prayer (petition, penitence and thanksgiving) presuppose that the relationship to be established, restored or acknowledged to exist between God and the person who prays, is one of agapeistic fellowship. Without this presupposition all three would become incoherent.

There is, however, one important difference between God and other people, which would seem to affect what we do when we express our gratitude to him in prayer. Since human agency is finite, only some events are brought about by what a human agent does. Other events take place without his agency and are beyond his control. This distinction does not apply to an omnipotent God. Nothing is beyond his control and no event could ever take place without his agency being involved.

No theist would deny that God is omnipotent, and that he could intervene to prevent any particular event's occurring, and that therefore his non-intervention is a necessary condition of each event ... Rome fell, we say, because God did not intervene to save it. But if Rome had not fallen, we should equally ascribe that to God's non-intervention, in the same way as we do ascribe its survival in previous centuries to God's forbearance. That is, whether Rome falls or not, God is the cause.[39]

But if God brings about *all* events, this presumably includes both good and evil, fortune and suffering. Does this entail that we should praise God for only some of the things he does and blame him for others? Should we be grateful only for some of the things he does for us but resentful for the evils he allows us to suffer? Indeed, resentment against God is not unknown among human beings. Not without reason J. Neville Ward claims that 'no person has ever been hated as much as God. There are many people who have no special quarrel with particular individuals but burn with a chronic resentment against the general treatment they have received at the hands of life. This is rage against God.'[40]

If, however, we are under some circumstances to consider resentment a legitimate response to God, does this not entail our accepting what D. Z. Phillips (following Simone Weil) calls a *naturalistic conception of God*,[41] i.e. the view that God's goodness depends upon and can be inferred from the way things go in the world? If things happen to go badly, the claim that God is good is falsified, and we have reason to resent what he does to us.

Gratitude to a naturalistic God is exactly like gratitude to a finite human person in always being correlated to resentment: I am grateful to you for doing this rather than that, but if you had done that instead I would have been resentful rather than grateful.

Is this view of God not unacceptable to the religious believer? Would a believer not want to claim that God's will is the ultimate standard of goodness in the light of which we determine whether the way things go is good or bad, whereas in the case of a naturalistic God the goodness of what he wills is determined in the light of the way things go? Should we not rather thank God for *everything* he does for us? Is D. Z. Phillips not correct in his view that 'when the believer thanks God for his creation, it seems to be a thanksgiving for his life as a whole, for everything, meaning the good *and* the evil within his life, since despite such evil, thanking God is still said to be possible. In devout religious believers, there seems to be no question of blaming God, but only of praising him.'[42] This seems to lead to the paradoxical conclusion that there can in fact be no evil. If God is always the cause of the way things go, and if he is to be thanked for whatever he does, this seems to entail that the way things go is *always* good and therefore a reason for gratitude towards God.

Maybe we should rather question the claim that God is always the cause of the way things go. In fact, does the claim that all events are brought about by God not make all talk of divine agency vacuous in the end? Is there not 'something vacuous in adding *Deo volente* to every prediction and every causal statement, because if it is to be *said* always, we could equally well *understand* it always, leaving it unsaid'?[43] On the other hand, this seems to entail a denial of divine omnipotence. If not all events are brought about by God, are some events then beyond his control? Is God then a finite agent like us?

We see, then, that divine agency is not like that of human persons. Since God is omnipotent, his agency is not finite like ours, and since he is perfectly good, he can be praised or thanked for all he does. His actions in fact never provide us with any reason for resentment. However, the dilemma we are discussing does not necessarily follow from these differences. In fact it can be avoided if we take seriously the complexities of causal agency concepts in general, as these apply to both God and human persons. In order to explain this point, we need again to pick up the strands of our discussion of these concepts in chapter 5, section 2 above.

There we introduced an important distinction which J. R. Lucas makes between the *complete cause* of an event (i.e. the complete set of causal conditions which together are sufficient to bring about the event), and the *most important cause* of the event (i.e. one or more of the causal factors included in the complete cause, and selected for a variety of reasons for special consideration). In cases where the agency of one or more persons is involved in bringing about an event, we usually select as most important the factor which we are to hold responsible, i.e. the factor which we decide to praise or blame for the event occurring. It is clear that not all the factors *necessary* for an event to occur are also held *responsible* for the event. If the floodlights go on when I turn the switch, I am held responsible for this rather than the technicians at the power station, even though their not striking at the time is an equally necessary condition for the floodlights going on.

How does this distinction help us with our problem about divine agency? Three points are important here. First, if God can intervene to prevent any particular event occurring, no event is possible unless God allows it to occur. Divine agency is therefore part of the complete cause of *every* event, and in this sense his agency is not finite like that of human persons. Secondly, if the theory of 'double agency' put forward in chapter 5, section 2 holds and God acts only through secondary causes, then God never lets his own agency be the complete cause of any event. His agency is one of the necessary conditions for every event, but not the only one, since he has decided to allow for secondary causes to co-operate with him in what he does. These secondary causes are independent originators of action with whom God has decided to share his power. This independence is of course *relative* and not absolute, since it is bestowed on the secondary causes by God who is able at any time to take back what he has given. The price for this, however, would be a deterministic universe in which divine agency is the complete cause of all events. This would be contrary to God's aim to create an orderly universe in which human persons can exist and freely co-operate with him in the realization of his purposes, a universe in which personal fellowship is possible between God and human persons. If this is the sort of universe God wants to bring about, he *logically* cannot do so if his agency is the complete cause of every event. Thirdly, if for every event divine agency is one but not the only necessary causal factor, then divine agency need not necessarily be the factor held responsible for every event. Since we praise him for the occurrence of some events, he is held responsible for their occurrence. But this does not exclude our ascribing responsibility for other events to other factors necessary for their occurrence. From the fact that God could have but did not prevent Auschwitz, it does not necessarily follow that we must hold him responsible for Auschwitz. We could also hold Hitler and his henchmen responsible, as in fact we usually do.

The question which arises here is: how are we to decide when we are to hold God responsible for an event and when we are to lay the responsibility elsewhere? How do we decide this in the case of human agents? There are various considerations which play a role in this sort of decision. First of all, we do not hold someone responsible for an event unless his agency is one of the necessary conditions for its occurrence. Thus we do not blame someone for an event which he could not have prevented because it was beyond his control. Secondly, even when he could have prevented an event, we do not hold someone responsible if he could not have foreseen the event in question. Thus we do not blame someone for unforeseeable effects of his actions. If the agent could have foreseen the effect but failed to do so because he did not bother to find out, we could blame him for *negligence*, i.e. 'voluntary unawareness of the nature of one's action'.[44] If the agent foresaw the *likelihood* of the effect, but did not care whether it occurred or did not bother to count the cost of its occurring, we could blame him for *recklessness*.[45] Obviously neither of these considerations are relevant in the case of God, since on the one hand divine agency in a necessary condition for the occurrence of every event, and on the other hand God in his omniscience can foresee all future possibilities and probabilities, as explained in chapter 3, section 3 above. Also God is never negligent or reckless in what he does because he knows the cost without first having to count it, and can therefore never be blamed for failing to count it or find it out.

There is a third consideration which applies also when somebody *knows* that his agency is a necessary condition for an event and that he is therefore able to prevent its occurrence. This is whether his action is *intended* to bring about the event in question. This needs some further explanation.

What do we mean by calling an action *intentional*? According to Anthony Kenny 'an agent intends an action if (*a*) he knows he is doing it and (*b*) does it because he wants to do it for its own sake or in order to further some other end'.[46] Kenny distinguishes such intentional actions from their foreseen consequences, concomitant effects and side effects. These are not intentional because bringing them about is not part of the reason for performing the action. The agent is of course able to avoid bringing them about, but only at the price of giving up the purposes or chosen means of which they are unintended consequences or effects.[47] Thus, although the agent does not *want* these in the strict sense of intending them, he does want them in a minimal sense of *consenting* to their occurrence.

> To say that an agent wants to do X, in this minimal sense, is merely to say that he does X consciously while knowing that it is in his power to refrain from doing X if only he will give up one of his purposes or chosen means. The wanting in question is mere willingness or consent: it is quite different from any feeling of desire, and may be accompanied with varying degrees of enthusiasm diminishing to reluctance and nausea.[48]

These distinctions are important in determining whether we are to blame (or praise) an agent when he knows that his agency is a necessary condition for the occurrence of an event, or whether we should rather hold responsible some other factor also necessary for the event to occur. Three sorts of cases should be distinguished here. First, as we have pointed out above, we only praise (or thank) someone for what he does intentionally and not for unintended consequences or effects of his actions. Especially when he only consents with reluctance or aversion to these consequences, it would be ironic to praise or thank him for the action which brings them about! Thus if your action was a necessary condition for the occurrence of some event of which I approve (or which is to my advantage), I will only praise (or thank) you if your action was intended to bring it about. Secondly, we could blame (or resent) what someone does, if he does it intentionally. Thus if your action is a necessary condition for the occurrence of some event of which I disapprove (or which is to my disadvantage), I will blame you (or be resentful to you) for bringing about the event if your action was *intended* to bring it about. Thirdly, in cases where it is not the purpose which your action is intended to achieve, but some unintended consequence or effect of your action of which I disapprove (or which is to my disadvantage), then I will only blame you (or be resentful to you) for consenting to this consequence or effect, if I disapprove of the fact that you let the achievement of your purpose prevail above avoiding the unintended consequence or effect of your action. Here, too, I am in fact disapproving (or resenting) the purposes which you *intentionally* try to realize in your action. In all cases, therefore, where your action is a necessary condition for an event occurring and you know that this is so, whether I am to praise or blame you (be grateful or resentful to you) for bringing about the event, depends on the *intention* with which you did what you did. Thus the English common law maxim *actus non facit reum nisi mens sit rea* (an act does not make someone guilty unless his mind is guilty too)[49] applies not only to blame but also to praise and thanksgiving.

In brief: praise or blame, gratitude or resentment, apply only to *actions* and not merely to *behaviour*. Since any adequate description of an action must include a reference to the intention with which the agent behaved the way he was seen to behave, we cannot simply equate someone's action with his observable behaviour. It follows that I can only praise or blame you (or be grateful or resentful) for what I perceive you to have done, if I know what your intention was in doing what you did. The problem is that I cannot infer this knowledge merely from what I perceive you to have done. I have rather to interpret what I perceive you doing in the light of my *prior knowledge* of your intentions.[50] But how do I get to know what you intend? There are mainly three ways in which I can know your intentions. First of all, I can know what you intend because you tell me. Secondly, I can infer your intentions from my knowledge of your character. Thus I presume that you are not acting out of character and that your intentions now are the same as I knew them to be when you were acting in similar circumstances in the past. Thirdly, I can infer your intentions from my knowledge of human nature or of the moral standards of the cultural community to which you belong. I presume that your intentions in doing what I perceive you to do are similar to those I know myself and other people (especially those belonging to the same cultural community as you do) to have when they act under similar circumstances. Thus in deciding whether to praise or blame you (or to be grateful or resentful) for an event, when your agency is a necessary condition for its occurrence, I have to *interpret* the occurrence in the light of what I believe to be your intentions. Although I can have grounds for this belief, it is never infallible and therefore I can always be mistaken in my praise or gratitude, blame or resentment.

How does this analysis of intentional action help us to understand what we do when we thank God? Three points are important here. First of all, even though God's agency is a necessary condition for every event, this does not entail that we have to thank him for every event. We thank him only for those events which he brings about *intentionally* and not for the unintended effects of his intentional acts. In other words, we thank him for events in which he realizes his purposes, and not for events which he permits even though they are contrary to his positive will. 'There is much that is contrary to God's positive will. He may permit, but he does not countenance or condone. Angels and men are in open rebellion against him.'[51]

Secondly, we can never blame God or resent what he does intentionally. The believer claims both that God's purposes (i.e. his positive will) are the ultimate standard of goodness, and that there is not the slightest likelihood that he would ever act out of character by deviating from his purposes.[52]

Thirdly, as St Paul enjoins us in I Thess. 5.18, we can give thanks to God whatever happens, even though we do not thank him *for* whatever happens.[53] Thus the believer would claim that an event is either intentionally brought about by God in order to realize his purposes, and then we could thank him for that; or it is an unintended consequence or effect of what God does intentionally. As such he consents to it even though he himself and we too might have to suffer as a result. In that case, the believer would say, we should also thank God for letting his perfect purposes prevail above avoiding these regrettable consequences.

E. G. Jay points out that the so-called Acts of the Martyrs, which recount the life and death of martyrs in the early church, report that 'much of the time of waiting before their execution they spent in prayer, and most of the Acts record that they died with words of praise and thanks to God upon their lips. These brave Christians were very conscious of the all-embracing providence of God, and their prayers are the expression of their faith.'[54] Obviously these martyrs were not masochists thanking God for intentionally letting them suffer! Rather they were thanking him for his 'all-embracing providence' in which he let his perfect purposes prevail, and for the sake of which they would gladly suffer martyrdom. They did not infer God's intentions from the suffering they experienced. Rather they interpreted their suffering in the light of their prior belief in God's intentions. In this sense D. Z. Phillips is correct in arguing that 'the relation between the assertion "God is good" and what happens is not one of inference'.[55] On the contrary, the believer claims that God is good because of his prior knowledge of God's intentions, and in the light of this knowledge he interprets what happens. But, as we have tried to show, the same applies to the intentional actions of human persons.

But how do we know God's intentions if we do not infer them from what happens? Above we noted three ways in which we get to know the intentions of other people: from what they tell us, from our knowledge of their character, and from our knowledge of the intentions of other people when acting in similar situations. The last of these does not apply in the case of God, since he is unique: his intentions and purposes are not analogous to those of other people, and cannot therefore be arrived at by analogy to those of other people. 'My thoughts are not your thoughts, and your ways are not my ways. This is the very word of the Lord' (Isa. 55.8). Also the first of these ways does not apply to God in the way it does to other people. You could inform me about your intentions in performing any specific act, but what would it be for God to inform me about his intentions with any specific event which he causes or allows? If I should have some experience which I take to be God telling me his intentions, how do I know that this is really God speaking and not merely my own imagination? If I should have such an experience (similar to those of the prophets in the Bible), I will have to test it in the light of the tradition of faith, which comprises the cumulative experience of the community of believers through the ages. But then our knowledge of God's intentions is more like the second of the three ways in which we know the intentions of other people: we infer God's intentions regarding specific events from our cumulative knowledge of his character and purposes. As we argued in chapter 5, section 3, the tradition of faith provides the believer with an interpretative framework in the light of which he decides what God's intentions could be with specific events.

There is one important difference here between God and other people. I might decide that your intentions in performing a specific act, are consistent with your character as I know it from long association with you. In this I could be mistaken, because you might always be acting out of character. God, however, never acts out of character. The believer claims that there is not the slightest likelihood that God will ever deviate from his purposes as these have been revealed to the community of faith through the ages.

It is clear that thanking (and praising) God presupposes an interpretation of life and experience in the light of faith. This kind of interpretation requires continual training because we are always in danger of succumbing to the alternative interpretation which makes us resentful rather than grateful. As J. Neville Ward explains:

> Christianity is a religion of happiness. It wants all men to be happy, to be able to live thankfully instead of resentfully. Resentful living is the alternative to thankful living, it is the condition of being against God and against life, unable to love either, and this is precisely the Christian idea of hell. We cannot of course always live thankfully, though this is the Christian ideal. We need help with the dark side of life which always provokes resentment. Most people cannot understand how one could possibly be thankful for what one dislikes in life, how resentment could possibly become thankfulness.[56]

Prayers of praise and thanksgiving not only presuppose an interpretation of experience in which, the believer claims, we see things as they are. They are themselves ways in which we are trained in seeing things as they are.

> The inflexible and demanding ego has been resisting the dismaying side of life so long that practice is necessary if it is ever

going to learn how to trust and obey. Such practice, at any rate as the saints have sketched it out, has always included regular exercises in the acceptance of disappointments and difficulties, and the seeking of God's will in them.[57]

In brief, interpreting all events in the light of faith, means seeing them as they are, and therefore acknowledging that in all events God maintains his fellowship with us. This is what it means to give thanks to God whatever happens.

In this chapter we have argued that prayer is a way in which the believer establishes, restores and acknowledges a relation of agapeistic fellowship with God. We have, however, ended this chapter on the same note as chapter 5 : prayer is not only a way of relating to God, but also a means of relating to the world, of seeing things as they are. This point may help us to understand the relation between prayer and the life of faith, between spirituality and morality. To this we now turn.

7

Praying
and Relating to the World

1. *Ora et labora*

In prayer a believer relates himself to God. We now have to see whether prayer is also connected with the way in which the believer relates himself to the world in his attitudes and actions. Does prayer have anything to do with the moral life? How we deal with this question depends on the sort of piety which we presuppose as context for prayer. Thus in pure mysticism 'the subject of prayer is exclusively, "God and the Soul", God the Highest Good, and the salvation and blessedness of the soul in the Highest Good'.[1] In his prayers the mystic does not try to relate to the world. He seeks rather union with God and *detachment* from the world.

> The praying mystic turns away from external reality, suppresses by force of will all ideas and emotions directed towards it and focusses his whole attention on the highest spiritual Reality, that is, on God.[2]

This is also reflected in the mystics view on morality.

> Mysticism does not value moral action as a thing good in itself, an absolute aim, that is, as the realization of values in personal and social life, but as a means to deaden the senses and suppress the emotions. Asceticism is the morality of the mystic, the purification of the soul's life.[3]

This emphasis on detachment from the world and union with

99

God alone, is not characteristic for the whole tradition of Christian piety. In fact, as J. Neville Ward points out, pure contemplative adoration directed to God alone can only be possible in the next life. Here and now we live in penultimacy, in temporality, and cannot avoid acting in relation to the world. Thus in this life prayer can only be justified if in some way it issues in works of love.

> The prayer that is prayer for its own sake, contemplation that enjoys its solitary communing with the ultimate but does not issue in love, seems like some absurd attempt to get out of time into eternity. This is really religious self-indulgence.[4]

This emphasis on the necessity for both prayer *and* works (*ora et labora!*) is found repeatedly throughout the history of Christian spirituality. Thus it is often stressed that St Paul's words 'pray without ceasing' (I Thess. 5.17) should not be taken as a call to continual praying and the exclusion of works. It is meant rather as an injunction somehow to relate all our works to our prayers. In this sense Origen argues that 'the man who links together his prayer with deeds of duty and fits seemly actions with his prayer is the man who prays without ceasing, for his virtuous deeds or the commandments he has fulfilled are taken up as a part of his prayer. For only in this way can we take the saying "Pray without ceasing" as being possible, if we can say that the whole life of the saint is one mighty integrated prayer.'[5]

What is the nature of this relation between prayer and works? Is it an *external* or contingent relation, or is it an *internal* or necessary one? Is prayer without works possible but wrong, or is it somehow absurd or logically incoherent? If, as Calvin claims, prayer is an 'exercise of faith',[6] there must be a close connection between the way prayer is related to works and the way faith or religious belief is related to morality. Let us therefore first examine this latter relation (chapter 7, section 2) before drawing some conclusions about the relation between prayer and the moral life (chapter 7, section 3).

2. *Religious belief and moral discourse*

Is there an *internal* relation between morality and religious belief, or is morality logically independent of religious belief? How we are to answer this question depends very much upon the *form of discourse* we choose when talking about the moral life. Thus we could express our moral commitments either in terms of moral *principles* or precepts or in terms of *models* and metaphors. This distinction needs some elaboration.

Morality does not merely deal in general with the things we do or the way we live, but more specifically with the things we *ought* to do and our *policy* for living. This policy is often expressed in terms of a code of moral *principles*. Such principles are rules or precepts in which some specific form of behaviour is described and the circumstances specified in which this form of behaviour is appropriate. Thus, for example, whenever circumstances C obtain (e.g. one is confronted by someone in need) one should always adopt form of behaviour B (e.g. offer assistence). A moral code consists of a coherent system of such principles which together express a policy for living. If we express our policy for living in this way, the relation between religion and morality would consist in the fact that religious believers try to live in accordance with the moral principles of a specific religious tradition. Thus Christians would try to live according to Christian principles. This way of stating the issue has two important implications.

1. On this view the relation between morality and religious belief becomes an *external* one, because there is nothing incoherent in accepting the moral principles and rejecting the religious beliefs. This is well illustrated by a recent controversy among Dutch Christian Democrats on the question whether it is necessary for someone becoming a member of the Christian Democratic Party that he should be a confessing Christian, or that it is sufficient for him to subscribe to the principles underlying the party programme without also being committed to the Christian faith. The implication is that the principles are not logically dependent on the faith and could also be accepted by people who are not committed Christians.

A believer might respond to this point by denying that his morality is independent of his faith, since the latter provides both the reason and the motivation enabling him to live according to his moral principles. He subscribes to these principles because they express the will of God and he is only able to live in accordance with them because the Spirit of God inspires him to do so.

True as this response may be, it does not entail that the believer's moral principles are *logically* dependent on his faith. Thus contemporary humanists would also subscribe to the moral principles of brotherly love, justice for all, human dignity, etc., without believing in a God who wills that they live according to these principles or inspires them to do so. They would derive their reasons and motivation from sources other than the Christian faith.

If in this way we define morality in terms of behaving in accordance with general moral principles, we cannot but agree with W. K. Frankena that 'those who think that morality is dependent on religion need not and do not always mean that it is logically dependent on religion. They may mean only that it is *causally* or *historically* dependent on religion, or that it is *motivationally* or psychologically dependent on religion.'[7]

2. If in this way the relation between religious belief and morality is an external one, it becomes difficult to maintain that the moral principles of the believer are *distinctive*. R. B. Braithwaite argues this point as follows.

> I take the fundamental moral teaching of Christianity to be the preaching of an agapeistic way of life. But a Jew or a Buddhist may, with considerable plausibility, maintain that the fundamental moral teaching of his religion is to recommend exactly the same way of life. How then can religious assertions be distinguished into those which are Christian, those which are Jewish, those which are Buddhist, by the policies of life which they respectively recommend if, on examination, these policies turn out to be the same?[8]

According to Braithwaite the difference between adherents of different faiths (and, we might add, non-religious views of life like Marxism, humanism, etc.) is not in the fundamental moral principles which they accept but in their ritual practices and in the stories (or sets of stories) which they associate with their moral commitments. The rituals and stories are useful as psychologically motivating techniques which strengthen the believer in his moral commitment, but they are nevertheless *externally* related to the moral principles.

We could agree with Braithwaite that religious beliefs and ritual practices (including prayers) provide the believer with reasons for accepting and a powerful motivation for living according to moral principles. However, as we argued in chapter 2, section 3, we cannot accept the sort of view which Braithwaite defends, that these beliefs (and the ritual practices connected with them) can be effective in providing moral motivation if we are to view them as 'stories' for which we make no truth claims. Even so, this does not affect the validity of Braithwaite's conclusion that the relation between religious beliefs and ritual practices on the one hand, and such general moral principles on the other, is motivational and not logical. As long as we define morality in terms of such general moral principles, it remains logically coherent for adherents of different religions and views of life to accept the same moral principles even though they do so for different reasons and with different sources of motivation.

However, we also talk about our moral life in terms of models and metaphors. Unlike Braithwaite's 'stories' these are not merely the imaginative means by which we could be motivated to accept moral commitments which are independently expressed. Rather they are themselves the means of expressing moral commitments. What does this imply for the relation between religious belief and morality?

In chapter 5, section 3 we pointed out that all experience involves interpretation: I experience x as y (the sound on the telephone as the voice of my friend, the image on the television as a picture of the Pope, etc.). Such interpretation is always aimed at our understanding of what we experience, and always involves some form of comparison: I understand x by comparing it to y and noticing that in some way it is like y. Interpretative comparison can take on many different forms and be aimed at different kinds of understanding.

One way in which we interpret our experience is by means of classification concepts: we note that x is like y because it belongs to the same class or category as y. We classify things intuitively (and often deliberately) in order to be able to cope with them. Thus we can cope with x in the same way as with y because it has the same characteristics as y, can be explained like y, can be treated like y, reacts in the same way as y, should be approached in the same way as y, or because the same attitude or course of action is appropriate in relation to it, etc. In this way classification is a basic function of our human form of life in the world.[9]

Apart from classification concepts, we also interpret our experience by means of metaphors and conceptual models. According to Sallie McFague:

A metaphor is seeing one thing *as* something else, pretending 'this' is 'that' because we do not know how to think or talk about 'this', so we use 'that' as a way of saying something about it. Thinking metaphorically means spotting a thread of similarity between two dissimilar objects, events, or whatever, one of which is better known than the other, and using the better-known one as a way of speaking about the lesser known.[10]

Such metaphorical thinking is fundamental to all scientific discovery and explanation. I discover how x works by noticing that it is like y – even though y is something very different. Thus, for example, Newton discovered something about the moon by noticing that it is like an apple – both being subject to gravity. However, scientists also use *conceptual models*, i.e. 'sustained and systematic metaphors',[11] in order to explore and explain the workings of physical phenomena. Thus they explain the behaviour of gasses by comparing it systematically with the behaviour of billiard balls, and they explain the behaviour of light rays in terms of waves or in terms of moving particles.[12]

Models and metaphors also play a basic role in religion and theology. Here, however, they are not introduced to help us discover or explain the way physical phenomena work, as in science. Religious models provide an understanding of the *meaning* or significance of our lives and of the world in which we live and in relation to which we act.[13] In this way they determine our actions and attitudes. Different religions and views of life provide their adherents with different models in terms of which life and the world can be understood, and which are definitive for the religions and views of life in question.

A similar point is made by Wittgenstein,[14] who argues that participating in religious belief is being able 'to use a picture'. In learning how to use the appropriate pictures in the appropriate ways, the believer must come to see which conclusions are to be drawn from the picture and which are not. In discussing this point in Wittgenstein, W. D. Hudson distinguishes two sets of conclusions which a believer must learn to draw.[15] First of all, he must learn to see how the expressions employed in the 'picture' resemble, and how they differ from their employment in ordinary non-religious contexts. Thus for example, if we use personal models in talking about God and his relation with human persons, we must determine the limits of the models: how is the relation between God and ourselves like and how is it unlike human relations? Here we have to sort out which implications of personal relation concepts, as these are used with reference to human relations, do, and which do not carry over to the way we are to understand the relation between God and ourselves. In previous chapters we have produced numerous examples of this sort of inquiry. Secondly, the believer must come to see what implications the models and metaphors have for his actions and attitudes as he comes to interpret his own life and the world in the light of them. Sorting out these two kinds of implications in a systematic way, is one of the important tasks in theological thought. Thus Sallie McFague argues that

> the central role of models in theology is to provide grids or screens for interpreting this relationship between the divine and the human . . . In order to interpret this relationship, conceptual clarity and precision is necessary: the structure implied in the relationship must be sorted out and its implications for personal, historical, social, and political life made manifest.[16]

Religious models determine the actions and attitudes to which the believer commits himself, mainly in two ways. First, in understanding himself and his own life in terms of the models, the believer discovers the role he has to play in life and action. Thus, 'man is a creature who makes pictures of himself and then comes to resemble the picture'.[17] Secondly, in interpreting the world in terms of the models, the believer comes to see which actions and attitudes are appropriate in relation to the world and in the various situations in which he has to act. These two points could be illustrated with reference to the Christian faith.

First of all, the Christian looks on his own life as a life lived *coram Deo* – in the presence of God. His role in life is therefore that of a child of God, who lives and acts in fellowship with God. In previous chapters we examined the implications of this role, and argued that it commits the believer to be available as secondary cause through whose agency God (as primary cause) can realize his intentions in the world. Secondly, as we tried to show in chapter 5, section 3 and chapter 6, section 3, the believer interprets the world in terms of the intentional agency of God. This entails that much of what he experiences in the world is for him an object of praise and thanksgiving to the God who brings it about. In this sense J. Neville Ward claims that thanksgiving is 'the essential Christian posture before experience'.[18] However, much else of what the believer experiences is seen as contrary to God's will and therefore to be opposed or changed. This entails a task which the believer is called upon to perform in fellowship with God. In these ways the models and metaphors in terms of which the believer interprets his life and the world, have a *commissive* force, since, in accepting the interpretation, the believer commits himself to specific attitudes and forms of action.

Do these models also have a *constative* force? Are they also claimed to be *true*? Or are they merely useful fictions for bringing order in the life of the believer, but not claimed to be factually true in any sense?[19] We have seen that philosophers like Braithwaite and Miles defend this kind of view, and, according to Hudson, what Wittgenstein seems 'at times to have come near to suggesting is that, because religious beliefs have commissive force, that somehow entitles us to by-pass the troublesome problem of their constative force'.[20] In discussing the views of Miles in chapter 2, section 3 above, we argued that the commissive force of religious beliefs presupposes the constative force. The actions and attitudes to which the believer commits himself in understanding his life in terms of these beliefs, become incoherent if he were to reject the factual claims involved in the beliefs. It would be incoherent to live my life as a life in the presence of God if I were to deny that there really is a God in whose presence I live.[21] In this way the actions are *internally* related to the beliefs: we cannot coherently commit ourselves to the former if we were to reject the truth of the latter.

We have tried to show that whether or not we could claim that the relation between morality and religious belief is an internal one, depends on the way in which we conceive of and talk about the moral life. If we express our moral commitments in terms of general moral principles, they appear to be externally related to religious beliefs. They could still be motivationally related to the beliefs but are not logically dependent on them. If, however, we express our moral commitments in terms of the models and meta-

phors of a specific religion, the relation turns out to be internal.
It would be logically incoherent to commit oneself to the way of
life expressed in these models, while refusing to believe that they
are somehow factually true. Logically I cannot live my life *coram
Deo* without believing that there is a God with whom I have a personal fellowship and with whom I am confronted in everything I do.

How are these two forms of moral discourse related? Do we
have to choose between them or are they in some way complementary? One possible answer would be to claim that religious
believers are committed to a moral life *coram Deo* which is internally related to their faith, and they should therefore express their
moral commitments in terms of the models of their faith. Non-
believers on the other hand, are committed to a morality which is
independent of religion and therefore state their moral views in
terms of general moral principles. Which form of moral discourse
we choose, therefore, depends on whether or not we are believers.
Arguing as a believer, Karl Barth seems to hold this sort of view
when he asserts that:

> Ethical theory is not meant to provide man with a programme
> the implementation of which would be his life's goal. Nor is it
> meant to present man with principles to be interpreted, applied,
> and put into practice ... Ethics exists to remind man of his
> confrontation with God, who is the light illuminating all his
> actions.[22]

The trouble with this view is that it does not square with the
way we in fact talk about morality. It is not true that only believers
express their moral commitments in terms of models and metaphors. Everybody does, even though not everybody would do so
in terms of the models of the Christian faith. Not everyone looks
on his own life as a life in fellowship with God. There is an infinite
variety of models in terms of which people interpret the meaning
of their own lives. Some relate their lives and actions to God,
others to Nirvana, the coming revolutionary struggle, the happi-
ness of mankind, the glory of the nation, or to some other ultimate
concern.[23] On the other hand, Christians, like everybody else,
also refer to moral principles and precepts when discussing moral
issues. Clearly we do not choose one of these two forms of moral
discourse to the exclusion of the other. In some way they are
complementary.

If religious beliefs are to have not merely a motivational relation to our moral commitments, but are also to determine the content of the commitments and the nature of the actions to which we are committed, how is expressing these commitments in terms of religious models *complementary* to expressing them in terms of moral principles? Does the use of models add something to our talk of moral behaviour in terms of principles? Ninian Smart makes the following suggestion.

> The superimposition of religious upon moral concepts ... gives the latter a different flavour: (*a*) because a moral action will have a double significance (not mere kindness, but consecrated kindness; not mere self-control, but a sacrifice, etc.); (*b*) because the solemnity of moral utterances becomes considerably increased: it is not merely that murder is wrong, but that life is *sacred*; a bad action is *sinful* and *impious*; discrimination against black folk in South Africa is not merely a great injustice, but it is (to quote a churchman's recent pronouncement) *blasphemy*; marriage is more than a fine institution, it is a *sacrament*.[24]

Thus Ninian Smart seems to say that we could all be committed to the *same* forms of moral behaviour as demanded by our common moral principles, and yet these forms of behaviour could have a quite different *flavour* depending on the religion (e.g. Christianity) or ideology (e.g. Marxism) or view of life (e.g. humanism) from which we derive the models which we *superimpose* on our moral principles.

This view is faced by two difficulties. First of all, it is not clear what is meant by the 'flavour' which the models give to the forms of moral behaviour described and recommended in our common moral principles. Does this mean merely that adherents of different religions, ideologies, etc., *feel* differently about the forms of behaviour they have in common? Or that their beliefs increase the *solemnity* of their moral commitments? I doubt whether many believers would recognize in this an adequate account of the bearing their religious beliefs have on the nature of their moral commitments!

A more serious difficulty has to do with the suggestion that adherents of different religions, ideologies, etc. are committed to the *same moral actions* (even though these have a different 'flavour' for each of them). Even when their *observable behaviour* is the same, this does not entail that they are *doing* the same. Action cannot be equated with observable behaviour because, as we argued in chapter 6, section 3, any adequate description of an *action* must include not only a reference to the observable behaviour of the agent but also of his *intentions* in behaving the way he does.

Stewart Sutherland explains this point with the following example.[25] The *observable behaviour* of Barry and Brendon is the same and can be described as 'driving lorryloads of food to the refugee camp'. Upon questioning, however, they describe what they *do* (i.e. their *actions*) in quite different ways. Barry says: 'In driving lorryloads of food to the refugee camp, I am meeting the needs of the politically oppressed masses, and in this way preparing the peasants physically for the coming revolutionary struggle, in accordance with the teaching of Mao.' Brendon, on the other hand, describes his action differently. He says: 'In driving lorryloads of food to the refugee camp, I am meeting the needs of my fellow creatures, and in this way partially realizing the Kingdom of God on earth in obedience to his will.' Although the observable behaviour of Barry and Brendon is the same, they are nevertheless performing very different actions, because the intentions with which they do what they do are quite different. These intentions cannot be adequately stated in terms of their observable behaviour alone. Although they both intend to feed the refugees, this is not a complete description of what they are doing. We must also include the higher level descriptions which they give to their actions, and which express both their higher level intentions and their beliefs about the way the world is which are presupposed by these intentions. Thus, in describing what they do in terms of their respective religious (or ideological) models, they are not merely ascribing a different 'flavour' to the *same* actions, but are claiming to perform quite different actions, with different higher level intentions which presuppose different and incompatible beliefs about the way the world is.

In the light of this example, it is clear why talking about the moral life in terms of behaviour principles makes the relation between religious belief and morality external, while talking in terms of religious models makes it internal. Behaviour principles describe and recommend forms of behaviour which could be commonly intended by adherents of different religions or ideologies, and do not, like the religious models, relate what is done to the higher level intentions and beliefs which differentiate the respective religions and ideologies.

Should we conclude from this that models and metaphors provide a more adequate form of moral discourse than general principles or precepts which could be commonly accepted by adherents of different religions? This conclusion would go too far. True, moral discourse in terms of models is more *basic* than that in terms of principles. We do not *superimpose* our models on our principles, but rather *abstract* out principles from our models. Nevertheless, we cannot do without this form of abstraction. We need discourse in terms of principles for various reasons, the two most important of which are the following.

In the first place, it is necessary in any society that people co-operate in common action even when they differ in their religious or ideological commitments. In order to reach agreement on such common action, it is necessary for them to abstract what is common in what they do, and argue about the advisability of that. In this sense we need common moral principles even when our intentions and beliefs (as expressed in our religious or ideological models) are different. Thus Barry and Brendon could only reach agreement about whether they should feed the refugees, if they stick to common moral principles and avoid arguing about whether they should do the will of God or follow the teaching of Mao.

Secondly, we need general moral principles for the sake of moral instruction. J. R. Lucas explains this point as follows.

We thus have to reduce the extreme complexity of the Christian life of love to relatively few principles, in much the same way as we have to reduce the complexity of English . . . composition to a few grammatical and syntactical principles when we want to teach someone. We need the moral law in something of the same way as we need grammar books. We formulate schematized and condensed sets of rules, because these can be taught to pupils fairly readily, and only when the pupil has mastered these can he develop the finer points of style. And just as we are careful to point out that to write grammatical English is not to have a good English style, so we also insist that to keep the commandments is not to live the Christian life. A man can keep all the rules of grammar, and yet write woodenly, and a man can keep the whole of the moral law and yet live a deadly life.[26]

We can conclude that, since religious belief provides the believer with the models in terms of which he understands the meaning of his life and of the world in relation to which he acts, the relation between such belief and the moral life of the believer is an internal one. What light does this throw on the relation between prayer and the moral life of the believer?

3. *Prayer and the moral life*

In chapter 6 we tried to show that in praying the believer establishes, restores, and acknowledges his fellowship with God. In this sense we can agree with Calvin in defining prayer as an 'exercise of faith'. In the light of our argument in the previous section, we can now say the same about the moral life of the believer. This life is the realization of the same fellowship. Thus, too, both prayer and the moral life of the believer are characterized by what Helen Oppenheimer calls 'triangulation',[27] since both involve three terms: God, the believer, and the world in which the believer lives and acts. In his moral life the believer relates to the world in fellowship with God, and in his prayer he seeks the fellowship with God in which he relates to the world. Furthermore, in chapter 2, section 3 we showed how prayer is internally related to religious belief. The former would be an incoherent activity if we were to reject the truth claims of the latter. In chapter 7, section 2 we saw that the same applies to the moral life of the believer. In both prayer and life it would be incoherent to relate ourselves to the world in fellowship with God, if we were to deny that there is a God who is related to the world and to ourselves.

Because of this very close connection between prayer and the moral life, it is not surprising that they have often been identified in some way or other. Thus, for example, in chapter 7, section 1 we quoted Origen who interpreted the moral life of the believer as itself a kind of prayer: 'the whole life of the saint is one mighty integrated prayer'.[28] From the opposite point of view one could also say that not only is the Christian life like a prayer, but prayer is also like the Christian life. Thus Ian Ramsey suggests that 'a time of prayer can be like the Christian life in miniature'.[29] Or one might say that prayer is an explicit expression of what is implicit in the whole of the Christian life. This is similar to what, according to E. G. Jay, Irenaeus held about eucharistic offerings:

> Irenaeus's meaning appears to be that the offerings made by Christians at the altar in the Eucharist must be thought of as particular and explicit expressions of what is implicit in the whole Christian life, namely service of God, without intermission directed to Almighty God in heaven.[30]

This identification of prayer and the Christian life would seem to make explicit prayer superfluous. If the whole life of the believer is a life of fellowship with God, why is it necessary in praying to repeat this whole in miniature? Why is it necessary to make explicit what is implicitly present in any case in the life of the believer? Should we not say with Emil Brunner that 'from the point of view of principle prayer ought not to be something alongside of other things, just as God is not something else alongside the world'?[31]

One might respond to this by referring to human imperfection. In a sense one might say that prayer will be superfluous in heaven, since there all life will naturally be fellowship with God. However, in this life we need continual training in order to live our lives in this way. Sanctification requires special effort. It does not come naturally to us. Thus Brunner argues that 'if we are bidden to observe fixed times for prayer, this is a concession to our human frailty, lest the exhortation to "pray without ceasing" come to mean – for us – that we "never" stop to pray at all.'[32] Similarly O. C. Quick writes that 'prayer represents the dedication of all human activity to God. It is the special part cut off, as it were, from our total activity in order that therein the dedication of the whole may be made self-conscious and thereby more complete.'[33]

There is much truth in this view. It is clear from our argument in previous chapters, that in different forms of prayer the believer consciously faces up to various aspects of his life in fellowship with God, and in this way trains himself for this life of fellowship. Thus in *petition* the believer faces up to his own dependence on God; in *intercession* he faces up to his own concern (or lack of concern) for the needs of others before God; in *penitence* he faces up to his own faults as sins in which his fellowship with God is being marred; in *dedication* he faces up to his own commitment (or lack of commitment) to doing God's will; in *praise* he faces up to looking on the world as an expression of God's goodness, holiness and glory; in *thanksgiving* the believer faces up to looking on his own capacities and opportunities and the fulfilment of his needs as gracious gifts from God. In this sense prayer is indeed a form of *meditation* in which the believer consciously faces up to the way in which he relates to God, to himself, to the world and to other people in his actions and attitudes. Thus in prayer the believer makes the dedication of his whole life to the fellowship of God (in the words quoted from Quick) 'self-conscious and thereby more complete'.

Although these remarks on the relation between prayer and the moral life, are true, they are also one-sided. Although prayer does further the moral life of the believer, its significance goes further than merely being a means to this end. In his prayer, as in his moral life, the believer is *practising* his fellowship with God, and not merely *practising for* it. The practice of prayer is not like practising swimming strokes without going into the water. In chapter 6 we showed that in praying the believer aims at *really* establishing, restoring and acknowledging his fellowship with God. Although this fellowship does issue in works, these are the effects, and not the purpose of praying. William Temple is right in emphasizing that 'the proper relation in thought between prayer and conduct is not that conduct is supremely important and prayer may help it, but that prayer is supremely important and conduct tests it'.[34]

In answer to the question we put at the beginning of this chapter, we can now say that the relation between the prayers and the moral life of the believer is an *internal* one. Prayer and the life of fellowship with God are impossible without each other. Thus it would be absurd to think that we could enter through prayer into fellowship with God, if this is not manifested in the life we live. On the other hand it is logically impossible to live a life of fellowship with God, if this fellowship is not established and re-established again and again, and this fact acknowledged in praise and thanksgiving. This is what we are doing when we pray.

NOTES

Notes

For details of the works referred to in these notes, see the bibliography which follows on pp. 129ff.

1. Introduction: Putting Prayer to the Test

1. See Lewis (2), 180f. for an interesting discussion of this problem.
2. Popper, 36.
3. Wisdom, 149.
4. For example, MacIntyre, 181, and Philips (2), 86f.
5. Ramsey (1), 71.
6. Popper, 36.
7. Popper, 37.
8. Calvin, III.20.52.
9. Lucas, 12.
10. Galton, 277.
11. Galton, 280f.
12. Galton, 282f.
13. Galton, 292f.
14. Galton, 293–94.
15. Galton, 282.
16. Baelz (1), 35.
17. A recent attempt at using modern methods of statistical inquiry to test the efficacy of prayer, also failed to produce significant results. See Joyce and Welldon, 367f.
18. The Archbishops' Commission on Divine Healing concluded: 'Scientific testing can be a valuable corrective of rash claims that healing, ordinary or extraordinary, has occurred and it may bring to light natural healing virtues in religious rites; but it is idle for the Church, or anyone else, to appeal to science to prove the reality of supernatural power or the truth of theology or metaphysic.' Quoted by Joyce and Welldon from *The Church's Ministry of Healing: Report of the Archbishops' Commission* (London 1958).
19. Appendix 3 to volume 39 of Aquinas (2).
20. Hardy, 285.

21. Quoted by William James in James, 446–47. James seems to agree with the view of Myers (James, 498), as does Hardy who defends a similar view in Hardy, chapter 10. See also Price for a defence of this way of explaining the efficacy of prayer.
22. Price, 53.
23. See for example Barth (1), III/3, 266f., and III/4, 97f., and Nédoncelle. For a contrary view, see Ritschl paragraph 79.
24. Calvin, III.20.
25. Ramsey (3), 22.
26. Calvin, III.20.51.

2. Therapeutic Meditation

1. Comte, 125. For Comte's views on the nature of prayer, see especially 105–9, 124–27.
2. Kant, 181. A contemporary defender of the Kantian view is Don Cupitt. See Cupitt, chapter 5, especially 68–69. 'In religion there is no independent being whose existence validates the practice of worship, just as in morality there is no independent being whose will validates the principles of morality. There does not need to be such an independent being, for the aim of worship is to declare one's complete and *disinterested* commitment to religious values. Belief in the God of Christian faith is an expression of allegiance to a particular set of values, and experience of the God of Christian faith is experience of the impact of those values on one's life.' Cupitt, 69.
3. Kant, 183f.
4. Kant, 181f.
5. Kant, 183n.
6. Kant, 185.
7. Kant, 183n.
8. Kant, 185.
9. Miles, 180f.
10. Miles, 184.
11. Miles, 186.
12. Miles, 186.
13. Miles, 187.
14. Elsewhere I have tried to develop an alternative criterion of 'factual content' which accounts more adequately for the factual claims of a metaphysical nature presupposed in religious belief. In the light of this criterion I try to show what these claims have in common with empirical claims, and how they differ. See Brümmer (2), chapters 17–19.
15. Penelhum, 284. This stoic view of prayer was defended in the French Enlightenment by Rousseau and others. See Heiler, 92.

16. Miles, 186.
17. Augustine, chapter 17.
18. Augustine, chapter 21.
19. Aquinas (2), 2a2ae.83.2.
20. Aquinas (2), 2a2ae.83.9.
21. Calvin, III.20.3. For a similar view in Luther, see his *Greater Catechism*, part 3.
22. Alhonsaari, 48f.
23. Kierkegaard, 51.
24. Hepburn, 148. D. Z. Phillips makes a similar point when he writes: 'It is essential for the believer to assert that he talks to someone other than himself when he prays. A conviction that one is talking to oneself is the death of prayer.' Phillips (1), 41. See also 64f. Phillips is often interpreted as defending a view like that of Kant or Miles. I do not think this is correct, even though the ambiguity of his argument does tempt one to read him in this way.
25. Price, 37f.
26. Van Buren, 190. For a critical analysis of Van Buren's views on this point, see Brümmer (2), 257–68.
27. Price, 38–39.
28. Penelhum, 284.
29. For an interesting discussion of the similarity between Kant's theory of religion and Bultmann's demythologization of the Christian faith, see De Vos, chapter 5.

3. Praying for Things to Happen

1. See Nédoncelle, 29f.
2. Heiler, 253.
3. Geach (1), 87.
4. Geach (1), 89f.
5. On prescriptives and their constitutive presuppositions, see Brümmer (2), 23f.
6. Descartes, 11f., 14f., 150f., 236f. See also Urban and Walton, 37–40. For a contemporary defence of the Cartesian position, see Plantinga, 92–126.
7. On asserting, see Brümmer (2), 26f.
8. On this point, see Geach (1), 90.
9. Aquinas (1), II.25.11.
10. Aquinas (1), II.25.15. See also Aquinas (2), 1a.25.4. For a full discussion, see Kenny (3), chapter 8.
11. Aquinas (1), II.25.12–14.

12. This suggests a solution to the so-called paradox of the stone: can God make a stone which is so heavy that he could not raise it? Both a positive and a negative answer to this question seems to entail a denial of God's omnipotence. If, however, God's omnipotence includes the ability to limit himself, we could affirm that God is able to make such a stone and thereby himself eliminate the possibility that he could raise it. On this paradox, see Urban and Walton, 131–68, and Swinburne, 152–58.

13. Aquinas (1), II.25.3–9.
14. Geach (4), 24–28.
15. Brümmer (3).
16. Swinburne, 182.
17. For this distinction, see Gibbs, 466–69.
18. Geach (1), 88–89. This point was already made by Origen: 'Just as, if anyone were to pray for the sun to rise, he would be deemed foolish for thinking that what would happen without his prayer comes to pass through his prayer, in the same way a man would be out of his wits who thought that those things which assuredly would happen even if he did not pray, come to pass because of his prayer.' Origen, V. 3 (Jay, 94–95).
19. Aquinas (2), 2a2ae.83.2.
20. Aquinas (2), 1a.42.1, and Aquinas (1), II.31–37. See also Penelhum, 259.
21. Origen, V. 6.
22. Geach (1), 71. See also 99f., and Geach (2), 321f.
23. Geach (1), 99.
24. Smith, 325f.
25. Geach (1), 98.
26. Augustine, chapter 17.
27. Swinburne, 231.
28. Smith, 328.
29. Geach (2), 323.
30. Geach (2), 323.
31. Lucas, 38f.
32. Origen, V. 6.
33. Boethius, V. 3. See also Pike (1).
34. Boethius, V. 6.
35. See Geach (2), 302f. for a similar critique of the more sophisticated but equally mistaken view that time is a fourth dimension on a par with the three dimensions of space.
36. For an extended critique of the view that God is timeless, see Pike (2).
37. Calvin, III.21.5.

38. Hebblethwaite (3), 441. See also chapter 3, section 1 above on God's ability to limit his own options.

39. Geach (4), 57–58. We shall have more to say about this metaphor in chapter 5, section 2 below.

40. Calvin, III. 20.3.

41. Aquinas (2), 2a2ae.83.2. Similarly Calvin writes that 'our prayers remind us that they [i.e. God's benefits] proceed from his hand'. Calvin, III.20.3.

42. Nédoncelle, 9. Nédoncelle gives a sensitive analysis of the difference between petition and command.

43. Augustine, chapter 17.

4. Prayer and the Goodness of God

1. Stump, 81–91. Stump states the issue in a more extended form than is done here. For a critical response to Stump, see Basinger (2), 25–41.

2. This view on divine goodness is defended in Helm (2). For a response to Helm, see Brümmer (4).

3. Stump, 85.

4. Aquinas (2), 2a2ae.83.2. For a contemporary defence of this position, see Helm (1), 454–61.

5. Augustine, chapter 21.

6. Evans, 170f.

7. Calvin, III.20.42.

8. Calvin, III.20.42.

9. Maclagan, 164.

10. Quoted by Maclagan, 164.

11. Oppenheimer, 57.

12. Stump, 89.

13. Bertocci, 495.

14. Price, 38.

15. Farmer, 263.

16. Bertocci, 493.

17. Oppenheimer, 63.

18. Farmer, 265.

19. Farmer, 265.

20. Burnaby (2), 234.

21. Farmer, 266–67. See also Kushner, chapter 7 for an interesting discussion on the limits of meaningful petition.

5. Prayer and the Agency of God

1. Swinburne, 139.

2. See Smart (1), chapter 2; Holland, 43–51; Hesse, 35–42.

3. For this view, see Penelhum, chapter 20.

4. Geach (1), 97.

5. See Hesse, 36f.

6. Burnaby (2), 232–33.

7. On this point see Brümmer (2), 120–21.

8. See Chisholm, 66–69.

9. Lucas, chapter 1.

10. Lucas, 13.

11. Lucas, 7.

12. Lucas's analysis is a distinct advance on the views of the originator of the term 'double agency', Austin Farrer. Farrer fails to provide an explanation of exactly how, on this theory, God's agency is related to that of man. Farrer ends with agnosticism on this point: 'Not knowing the modality of the divine action we cannot pose the problem of their mutual relation' (Farrer, 66). Maurice Wiles agrees with this agnosticism: 'We do not understand the modality of the divine action in a way which enables us to define its relation to our finite human acting' (Wiles (2), 248). For lack of a better explanation, Wiles settles for a view which he admits 'is deistic in so far as it refrains from claiming any effective causation on the part of God in relation to particular occurrences' (Wiles (1), 38). On Farrer's position impetratory prayer remains mysterious, whereas that of Wiles makes it meaningless.

13. Basinger (1), 509. Basinger's essay is a critique of Geach's metaphor comparing God to a supreme Grand Master in chess. As we pointed out in chapter 3, section 3, Geach introduces this metaphor in order to explain his thesis that 'God knows the future by *controlling* it'.

14. Lucas, 30, 33.

15. On this way of distinguishing between being God's agents and being God's instruments, see Oman chapter 3.

16. Farrer, 110. See also Hebblethwaite (2), 225.

17. Hebblethwaite (1), 543. In this way the claim that an event is an act of God in answer to prayer, is not a straightforward *empirical claim* (see chapter 2, section 1 above) which can be subject to some sort of *empirical test* (see chapter 1, sections 2, 3 and 4 above).

18. On this distinction see Holland.

19. According to T. S. Eliot, 'we found our belief in the miracles on the Gospel, not our belief in the Gospel on miracles'; Eliot, 156.

20. Elsewhere I have discussed the difficulties involved in the claim that God can be known from his works. See Brümmer (2), 270–75.

21. Wittgenstein (1), 194.

22. See chapter 4 of Alhonsaari on prayer and dialogue.

23. See chapter 3 of Mavrodes for a useful analysis of the concept of experience, and an explanation of the way in which all experience

involves interpretation. See also chapters 2 and 5 of Donovan, chapter 2 of McFague, and Brümmer (1).

24. For this term, see Hick, chapter 3.

25. Calvin, I.6.1. See also the words of Charles M. Wood: 'Thus to describe an occurrence as an act of God is not to indulge in a pious overdescription of the events involved, justified perhaps by their impressiveness. It is instead to place the occurrence within a different context of description, on the basis of the agent's own self-disclosure. It is to acknowledge a God who not only acts, but also speaks.' Wood, 284. We will return to this point in chapter 6, section 3 below.

26. Alhonsaari, 47–48.

27. Drury, chapter 1.

28. Thus also Peter Martyr Vermilius: 'This is the character of the sons of God, that they frequently take time for prayers; for that is what it means to perceive the providence of God.' Quoted by Albrecht Ritschl in Ritschl, 282.

29. Lucas, 38.

6. Praying and Relating to God

1. Heiler, chapters 6–9.

2. Heiler, 227.

3. Heiler, 136.

4. Heiler, 169.

5. Heiler, 169–70.

6. Heiler, 217

7. Heiler, 197.

8. Heiler, 275.

9. Heiler, 173f.

10. Quoted in Heiler, 190.

11. Heiler, 177.

12. Heiler, 358.

13. Heiler, 174.

14. Heiler, 278.

15. Heiler, 192.

16. Drury, 66.

17. Drury, 68. See also Nédoncelle, 48f.

18. Quick, 92–93.

19. For a more detailed analysis of the differences between forgiveness and condonation, see Downie. See also Lucas, 78f. An example of someone who interprets forgiveness in terms of condonation or pardon, is Alhonsaari. See Alhonsaari, 161f.

20. Strawson, 6.

21. Burnaby (1), 87.

22. For a more detailed analysis of the differences between penitence and penance on the one hand, and punishment on the other, see Lucas, 80f.

23. Minas, 32.

24. See Lampe, Lucas, chapter 10, Burnaby (1), and Ramsey (2), 28–60.

25. Baelz (1), 107.

26. Kierkegaard, 50.

27. Ward, 43.

28. Lewis (1), 33.

29. Kierkegaard, 51. See also Phillips (1), chapter 4.

30. Maclagan, 161.

31. Brümmer (3). See also chapter 3, section 2 above.

32. Phillips (1), 63.

33. Ward, 46.

34. Strawson, especially 4–20.

35. Strawson, 5.

36. Phillips (1), 96.

37. Phillips (1), 96.

38. Alhonsaari, 173.

39. Lucas, 9.

40. Ward, 65.

41. Phillips (1), 98.

42. Phillips (1), 97.

43. Lucas, 9.

44. Kenny (2), 6.

45. Kenny (2), 63.

46. Kenny (1), 56.

47. Kenny (1), 57–59.

48. Kenny (2), 51.

49. For an interesting discussion on the principle of *mens rea*, see Kenny (2), chapters 1 and 3.

50. On this point, see also Wood.

51. Baelz (1), 81.

52. See Brümmer (3).

53. The view of D. Z. Phillips on thanking God, appears paradoxical because he does not seem to make this distinction. See Phillips (1), chapter 5.

54. Jay, 18.

55. Phillips (1), 97.

56. Ward, 21–22.

57. Ward, 65.

Notes

7. Praying and Relating to the World

1. Heiler, 191.
2. Heiler, 180.
3. Heiler, 157–58.
4. Ward, 31.
5. Origen, XII.2 (Jay, 114–15). See also Jay, 68 for comments.
6. Calvin, III.20.
7. Frankena, 15.
8. Braithwaite, 243–44.
9. See Brümmer (2), 56f. on the connection between classification and forms of life.
10. McFague, 15. McFague's book provides a more detailed analysis than is possible here of the interpretative function of metaphors and models, especially in religion and theology.
11. McFague, 67.
12. See Barbour, 30 on the billiard ball model and Barbour, 71f. on the wave and particle models in light theory. Barbour's book provides a useful comparison between the use of models in science and religion.
13. On this sense of 'meaning' see chapter 9 of Brümmer (2).
14. Wittgenstein (2).
15. Hudson, 38f.
16. McFague, 125.
17. Murdoch, 122.
18. Ward, 20.
19. Similar questions also arise with reference to the models used in scientific inquiry, and realists differ from instrumentalists as to the answers. See Barbour chapter 3.
20. Hudson, 44.
21. See Brümmer (2), chapters 17–19. See also chapter 2, section 3 above.
22. Barth (2), 86.
23. See Christian, chapter 9.
24. Smart (2), 24.
25. Sutherland, 160f.
26. Lucas, 100.
27. Oppenheimer, 61.
28. Origen, XII.2.
29. Ramsey (3), 22.
30. Jay, 17.
31. Brunner, 311.
32. Brunner, 311.
33. Quick, 289.
34. Quoted in Ward, 30.

BIBLIOGRAPHY

Bibliography

Alhonsaari, A., *Prayer. An Analysis of Theological Terminology*, Helsinki 1973.

Aquinas, Thomas (1), *On the Truth of the Catholic Faith (Summa Contra Gentiles)*, Book II, trans. J. F. Anderson, New York 1957².
(2), *Summa Theologiae* (Blackfriars edition), vol. 5, London 1967; vol. 39, London 1964.

Augustine, Aurelius, *Letters*, trans. J. G. Cunningham. In vol. I of *A Select Library of the Nicene and Post-Nicene Fathers of the Christian Church*, ed. Philip Schaff, Grand Rapids 1979 (reprint).

Baelz, P. R. (1), *Prayer and Providence*, New York 1968.
(2), *Does God Answer Prayer?*, London 1982.

Barbour, I. G., *Myths, Models and Paradigms*, London 1974.

Barth, K. (1), *Church Dogmatics*, ed. G. W. Bromiley and T. F. Torrance, vol. III/3 and III/4, Edinburgh 1961.
(2), *The Humanity of God*, trans. Th. Wieser, Richmond 1963.

Basinger, D. (1), 'Human Freedom and Divine Providence: some New Thoughts on an Old Problem', *Religious Studies* 15, 1979, pp. 491–510.
(2) 'Why Petition an Omnipotent, Omniscient, Wholly Good God?' *Religious Studies* 19, 1983, pp. 25–41.

Bertocci, P. A., *Introduction to Philosophy of Religion*, Englewood Cliffs NJ 1951.

Boethius, *The Consolation of Philosophy*, trans. W. V. Cooper, with an introduction by I. Edman, New York 1943.

Braithwaite, R. B., 'An Empiricist's View of the Nature of Religious Belief', in *The Existence of God*, ed. J. Hick, New York 1964, pp. 229–52.

Brümmer, V. (1), 'Lyttkens on Religious Experience and Transcendence', *Religious Studies* 15, 1979, pp. 221–25.
(2), *Theology and Philosophical Inquiry*, London 1981.
(3), 'Divine Impeccability', *Religious Studies* 20, 1984, pp. 203–214.
(4), 'Paul Helm on God and the Approval of Sin', *Religious Studies* 20, 1984, pp. 223–226.

Brunner, E., *The Divine Imperative*, trans. O. Wyon, London 1949³.

Bibliography

Buren, P. M. Van, *The Secular Meaning of the Gospel*, London, 1965².

Burnaby, J. (1), *Christian Words and Christian Meanings*, London 1955.
(2), 'Christian Prayer', in *Soundings*, ed. A. R. Vidler, Cambridge 1962, pp. 221–37.

Calvin, J., *Institutes of the Christian Religion*, vol. II, trans. H. Beveridge, London 1953.

Chisholm, R. M., *Person and Object*, London 1976.

Christian, W. A., *Meaning and Truth in Religion*, Princeton 1964.

Comte, A., *The Catechism of Positive Religion*, London 1858.

Cupitt, D., *Taking Leave of God*, London 1981.

Descartes, R., *Philosophical Letters*, trans. A. Kenny, Oxford 1970.

Donovan, P., *Interpreting Religious Experience*, London 1979.

Downie, R. S., 'Forgiveness', *Philosophical Quarterly* 15, 1965, pp. 128–34.

Drury, J., *Angels and Dirt. An Enquiry into Theology and Prayer*, London 1972.

Eliot, T. S., *Selected Prose*, ed. J. Hayward, Aylesbury 1953.

Evans, D. D., *The Logic of Self-Involvement*, London 1963.

Farmer, H. H., *The World and God*, London 1939³.

Farrer, A., *Faith and Speculation*, London 1967.

Fosdick, H. E., *The Meaning of Prayer*, London 1927.

Frankena, W. K., 'Is Morality Logically Dependent on Religion?', in *Divine Commands and Morality*, ed. P. Helm, Oxford 1981, pp. 14–33.

Galton, F., *Inquiries into the Human Faculty and its Development*, London 1883.

Geach, P. T. (1), *God and the Soul*, London 1969.
(2), *Logic Matters*, Oxford 1981².
(3), 'The Future', *New Blackfriars* 54, 1973, pp. 208–18.
(4), *Providence and Evil*, Cambridge 1977.

Gibbs, B., 'Can God Do Evil?', *Philosophy* 50, 1975, pp. 466–69.

Hardy, A., *The Living Stream*, London 1965.

Hebblethwaite, B. L. (1), 'Austin Farrer's Concept of Divine Providence', *Theology* 73, 1970, pp. 541–51.
(2), 'Providence and Divine Action', *Religious Studies* 14, 1978, pp. 223–36.
(3), 'Some Reflections on Predestination, Providence and Divine Foreknowledge', *Religious Studies* 15, 1979, pp. 433–48.

Heiler, F., *Prayer*, trans. S. McComb, London 1958².

Helm, P. (1), 'Omnipotence and Change', *Philosophy* 51, 1976, pp. 454–61.
(2), 'God and the Approval of Sin', *Religious Studies* 20, 1984, pp. 215–222.

Bibliography

Hepburn, R. W., 'Poetry and Religious Belief', in *Metaphysical Beliefs*, ed. A. MacIntyre, London 1957, pp. 83–166.

Hesse, M., 'Miracles and the Laws of Nature', in *Miracles*, ed. C. F. D. Moule, London 1965, pp. 35–42.

Hick, J., *God and the Universe of Faiths*, London 1973.

Holland, R. F., 'The Miraculous', *American Philosophical Quarterly* 2, 1965, pp. 43–51.

Hudson, W. D., 'Some Remarks on Wittgenstein's Account of Religious Belief', in *Royal Institute of Philosophy Lectures Volume II: Talk of God*, London 1969, pp. 36–51.

James, W., *The Varieties of Religious Experience*, Glasgow 1982[11].

Jay, E. G., See Origen.

Joyce, C. R. B. and Welldon, R. M. C., 'The Objective Efficacy of Prayer', *Journal of Chronic Diseases* 18, 1965, pp. 367–77.

Kant, I., *Religion within the Limits of Reason Alone*, trans. Th. M. Greene and H. H. Hudson, New York 1960.

Kenny, A. (1), *Will, Freedom and Power*, Oxford 1975.
   (2), *Freewill and Responsibility*, London 1978.
   (3), *The God of the Philosophers*, Oxford 1979.

Kierkegaard, S., *Purity of Heart*, trans. D. V. Steere, New York 1956.

Kushner, H. S., *When Bad Things happen to Good People*, London 1982.

Lampe, G. W. H., 'The Atonement: Law and Love', in *Soundings*, ed. A. R. Vidler, Cambridge 1962, pp. 175–91.

Lewis, C. S. (1), *Letters to Malcolm: Chiefly on Prayer*, London 1964.
   (2), *Christian Reflections*, Glasgow 1981.

Lucas, J. R., *Freedom and Grace*, London 1976.

McFague, S., *Metaphorical Theology*, London 1982.

MacIntyre, A., 'The Logical Status of Religious Belief', in *Metaphysical Beliefs*, ed. A. MacIntyre, London 1957, pp. 167–211.

Maclagan, W. G., *The Theological Frontier of Ethics*, London 1961.

Mavrodes, G. I., *Belief in God*, New York 1970.

Miles, T. R., *Religion and the Scientific Outlook*, London 1959.

Minas, A. C., 'God and Forgiveness', in *Contemporary Philosophy of Religion*, ed. S. M. Cahn and D. Shatz, New York 1982, pp. 32–45.

Murdoch, I., 'Metaphysics and Ethics', in *The Nature of Metaphysics*, ed. D. F. Pears, London 1962[3], pp. 99–123.

Nédoncelle, M., *The Nature and Use of Prayer*, trans. A. Manson, London 1964.

Oman, J., *The Paradox of the World*, Cambridge 1921.

Oppenheimer, H., 'Petitionary Prayer', *Theology* 73, 1970, pp. 54–64.

Origen, *Treatise on Prayer*, trans. E. G. Jay, London 1954.

Penelhum, T., *Religion and Rationality*, New York 1971.

Phillips, D. Z. (1), *The Concept of Prayer*, London 1968[2].
   (2), *Faith and Philosophical Enquiry*, London 1970.

Bibliography

Pike, N. (1), 'Divine Omniscience and Voluntary Action', *Philosophical Review* 64, 1965, pp. 27–46.

(2), *God and Timelessness*, London 1970.

Plantinga, A., *Does God Have a Nature?* Milwaukee 1980.

Popper. K. R., *Conjectures and Refutations*, London 1969³.

Price, H. H., *Essays in the Philosophy of Religion*, Oxford 1972.

Quick, O. C., *Essays in Orthodoxy*, London 1916.

Ramsey, I. T. (1), *Religion and Science: Conflict and Synthesis*, London 1964.

(2), *Christian Discourse*, London 1965.

(3), *Our Understanding of Prayer*, London 1971.

Ritschl, A., *Three Essays*, Philadelphia 1972.

Smart, N. (1), *Philosophers and Religious Truth*, London 1964.

(2), 'Gods, Bliss and Morality', in *Christian Ethics and Contemporary Philosophy*, ed. I. T. Ramsey, London 1966, pp. 15–30.

Smith, T. P., 'On the Applicability of a Criterion of Change', *Ratio* 15, 1973, pp. 325–33.

Strawson, P. F., *Freedom and Resentment and Other Essays*, London 1974.

Stump, E., 'Petitionary Prayer', *American Philosophical Quarterly* 16, 1979, pp. 81–91.

Sutherland, S. R., 'Religion, Ethics and Action', in *The Philosophical Frontiers of Christian Theology*, ed. B. Hebblethwaite and S. Sutherland, Cambridge 1982, pp. 153–67.

Swinburne, R., *The Coherence of Theism*, Oxford 1977.

Urban, L. and Walton, D. N. (eds), *The Power of God*, New York 1978.

Vos, H. de, *Kant als Theoloog*, Baarn 1968.

Ward, J. N., *The Use of Praying*, London 1967.

Wiles, M. (1), *The Remaking of Christian Doctrine*, London 1974.

(2), 'Farrer's Concept of Double Agency', *Theology* 84, 1981, pp. 243–49.

Wisdom, J., *Philosophy and Psycho-Analysis*, Oxford 1953.

Wittgenstein, L. (1), *Philosophical Investigations*, trans. G. E. M. Anscombe, Oxford 1958².

(2), *Lectures and Conversations on Aesthetics, Psychology and Religious Belief*, ed. C. Barrett, Oxford 1966.

Wood, C. M., 'The Events in which God Acts', *The Heythrop Journal* 22, 1981, pp. 278–84.

Young, R., 'Petitioning God', *American Philosophical Quarterly* 11, 1974, pp. 193–201.

INDEX

Index

Index

Index